by the same author

DANCES OF ENGLAND AND FRANCE 1450–1600

DANCES
OF SPAIN AND ITALY

FROM 1400 TO 1600

BY

MABEL DOLMETSCH

DA CAPO PRESS • NEW YORK • 1975

A DA CAPO PRESS REPRINT

Library of Congress Cataloging in Publication Data

Dolmetsch, Mabel.
    Dances of Spain and Italy from 1400 to 1600.

    Reprint of the 1954 ed. published by Routledge and
Kegan Paul, London.
    Bibliography : p.
    Includes index.
    1. Dancing—Spain. 2. Dancing—Italy. I. Title.
GV1618.D63 1975   793.3'1   74-28450
ISBN 0-306-70726-8

This Da Capo Press edition of *Dances of Spain and Italy* is an un-
abridged republication of the first edition published by Routledge and
Kegan Paul Ltd. in London in 1954. It is reprinted with the permission
of Miss Cecile Dolmetsch.

Published by Da Capo Press, Inc.
A Subsidiary of Plenum Publishing Corporation
227 West 17th Street, New York, N.Y. 10011

In Memory of
ARNOLD DOLMETSCH

Contents

Illustrations

Introduction

THE combined influences of territorial conquest and royal alliances which gradually brought about an interchange and blending of the social arts of England and France during the medieval and Renaissance periods, find their parallel in a similar association between Spain and Italy. This comparison refers to the northern half of the Spanish Peninsula, the artistic culture of the South having throughout the Middle Ages intermingled with that of North Africa, supplemented by contributions from the Arab dominions farther east.

By contrast, the music and dancing of Northern Spain may be considered as of European growth; and the happy circumstance of this intercourse between Spain and Italy has secured for us some valuable documentary evidence of ancient Spanish dances, of which otherwise we should have had but a vague idea.

In Spain, owing to centuries of warfare, the career of arms (apart from the religious calling) came to be esteemed beyond all others. Consequently it was mainly amongst the clergy that there existed men with sufficient learning and leisure to treat of artistic and intellectual subjects. These do not appear to have been moved to write about the Dance; or else their writings have not been handed down to us. Hence, beyond certain literary allusions by Cervantes and a short technical treatise of the early seventeenth century,[1] we are indebted to France and, above all, to Italy for our precise knowledge of the medieval and Renaissance dances of Northern Spain. Many of these surviving examples are of the courtly type; but certain of a more popular character have fortunately been preserved. On these last the ebb and flow of Moorish domination has left some traces in the guise of steps, gestures and rhythms of a wilder, fiercer stamp, suggestive of an African origin.

The treatises (French and Italian) of this period make no mention of the use of *castañets* (now a feature of Spanish dancing). This is understandable when we realize that the performers frequently danced hand in hand, either in couples or in long lines or circles, and again with linked arms, or joined, raised hands in wheeling movements. Such grouping would be incompatible with the free handling of *castañets*; and the rhythmic emphasis where needed was provided by one of the *sonatori* on some instrument of percussion.

The Italian masters were pre-eminent in the art of detailed description of the correct

---

[1] *Discursos sobre el Arte del Dançado*, Juan de Esquivel Navarro, 1647.

technique and style of performance, conveying therein an impression of superfine grace and finish. Their system is more elaborate than that of the French; for, with them, the basic steps are subject to many modifications, all of which are classified under distinguishing names. The convenient tablature used in France is replaced by these multifarious names; and, although at first sight this method appears more complicated, it has advantages from the interpretative standpoint.

Thus the two systems help and complete each other, the French method, as exemplified by Arbeau, facilitating an instantaneous grasp of the structure of a dance, whereas that of the Italians conveys an idea of the subtleties of style and histrionic effects which reveal its individual character.

Chapters I and II, being principally of historical interest, may be passed over without loss by those whose main interest lies in the performance of these dances.

CHAPTER I

Historical Survey of the Bassa Danza

ITALY, in the course of the fifteenth century, produced several important dance treatises, which have been preserved in various public libraries. Five of these manuscripts consist of individually distinct versions of an elaborate work by a highly intellectual Jewish author named Guglielmo Ebreo of Pesaro. The most perfect of these is a superb manuscript in the Paris Bibliothèque Nationale (Fonds it. 973). Another close copy of this version is also preserved in the Bibliothèque Nationale (Fonds it. 476), and contains some additional matter of minor importance. The authorship is herein ascribed, strange to say, to one Giovanni Ambrosius, who was probably responsible for the additional remarks. One copy has survived of a treatise by the fifteenth-century poet Antonio Cornazano, who approaches the subject from a rather different angle and gives some technical details not touched on by Guglielmo. This manuscript is in the Vatican Library (codex Caponiano No. 203).

All of the above-mentioned works are avowedly based upon one original treatise by a greatly revered master named, variously, Domenico de Piacenza, Domenichino piacentino, and (owing to his sojourn at the court of the Marquess Leonello d'Este) Domenico da Ferrara. From this great genius the other three writers claim to have learned the art of dancing.

Before proceeding further with this subject I would like to draw attention to a masterly analysis of these manuscript treatises by Dr. Otto Kinkeldey, of New York, contributed under the title *A Jewish Dancing Master of the Renaissance*, to a memorial volume: *Studies in Jewish Bibliography and related subjects: in memory of Soloman Freidus.*[1] It is not my intention to go over the same ground, already so admirably covered by this scholarly writer, but to approach the subject from the standpoint of the practitioner who has spent some years in historical research. Thus I hope to throw light on certain theoretical obscurities

[1] Published by the Alexander Kohut Memorial Foundation, New York, 1929.

I

and to establish a sequence from Italian and Spanish medieval dancing to that of the late Renaissance, an extremely rich period in Spain and Italy.

Of the above-mentioned parent treatise there exists only a transcript, itself very ancient, now preserved in the Paris Bibliothèque Nationale (Fonds it. 972). Herein the author of the treatise is spoken of in the third person; but this may be due to a personal idiosyncrasy of Domenichino.

The title-page of this manuscript is missing; and near the top of the first page of text there has been written in a cursive hand 'De arte saltandj & choreas discendj'. Below this Latin title is the Italian translation: 'De la arte di Ballare et danzare', while, above the writing, there appears in Roman characters mm cccc XVI. Assuming that the double 'm' represents a capital letter, I conclude that 1416 is the date of Domenichino's treatise. The language and style are remote and the orthography very near to the original Latin, all of which points lend support to the assumption of this early date. Let us therefore go straight to the fountain-head.

The master begins by defending the nobility and virtue of the Dance and also the moral purity of supple, rhythmic bodily movement, in sympathy with that of the feet, against those who stigmatize such movements as lascivious. This interesting prologue is a vivid revelation of the histrionic character of fifteenth-century dancing as understood by the great exponents of Northern Italy. In order to assist the reader to a ready comprehension, I will divide my translation into paragraphs, with added punctuation:

'Rendering thanks to the great god of the intellectual faculties, which by his grace alone are inspired and by him alone bestowed: to him be honour and glory for all his works, both intellectual and moral.

'And the respected and noble cavalier, Messer Domenighino piacentino, desiring to produce a treatise, prayed with great reverence to him who, by his sacred humanity, ever deigned to succour the aforesaid, accomplishing and bringing this matter to a successful issue.

CONCERNING BODILY MOVEMENT

'And nevertheless there have been many who were opposed to this ardent and free mobility exercised with great subtlety and discernment, as being lascivious and wanton. But the author argued against this with righteous zeal [*in lo zelo del heticha*], saying that all things are liable to corruption and degeneration if they are employed indiscreetly: that is, with exaggeration. It is moderation that conserves. Well did the wise Aristotle treat somewhat of bodily movements, practised with virtuous ardour, without which it would never be possible to know how to convey with subtlety the exquisite shades of meaning that can be expressed by this bodily mobility, moving from place to place with measure, memory, agility and fluent grace [*maniera*]: measure of the terrain assisting and inspiring the body with sensitive alertness [*fantasmata*], himself thus discoursing and putting forth

Gentleman inviting Lady to Dance

arguments both good and true in favour of this art and this gentle expressiveness, with as much understanding and enthusiasm as is possible. And note, galante, that by the exercise of bodily mobility, avoiding all extravagance, this gentle art, I say, will have within itself a natural beauty and much decorum withall.'

Domenichino next explains that it is useless for a person lacking this suppleness of body, or one who is in any way handicapped by some deformity, to undertake to become a dancer, beauty and physical aptitude being of primary necessity. Yet, he says, beauty alone will not suffice; but there must also be an intellectual grasp of the scientific principle underlying the structure of the dance. 'I tell you', he continues, 'that the foundation of this is measure, including all rapid and all slow movements, according to the music. Besides this, it is necessary to have a great and profound memory, which applies to all bodily movements, both natural and accidental, that appertain to every action according to the form in which dances are composed. And note that, beyond all this, it is needful to have a consummate and easy agility and bodily grace. Yet beware of carrying this agility and demonstrative gesture to extremes. Be temperate in your movements so that they do not become either exaggerated or too restrained, but are as suave as the aspect of a gondola which, propelled by two oars over the wavelets of a calm sea, according to its nature, slowly rises on the said wavelets and quickly dips again: always observing the fundamental principle which is measure, this being a slackening of speed compensated with great rapidity.'

Concerning *measure*, he says that, apart from musical measure, there is another kind concerned with grace of movement and deportment and also a just appraisement of the space at the dancer's disposal (*el terreno*), which kind of measure demands adroitness and sensibility, enabling the dancer to proportion his movements from head to foot and to avoid all uncouth extremes.

'And also I tell you, my son, that in this *métier* which you wish to learn there is need to dance with alert spontaneity [*fantasmata*]; and note that this *fantasmata* consists of bodily rapidity motivated by an understanding of the [rhythmic] measure described above, whereby, during each bar one gives an instant's pause as though having seen the Medusa's head, as says the poet: that is to say that, having made a movement, one is in that instant as though turned to stone, and in the next instant takes wing like the falcon, which joyous movement is in accordance with the above rule, that is a combining of measure, memory, *maniera* [graceful expression] and measure of the terrain and the aria.' With regard to this last, it is stated that there must be concordance among the dancers and a correlated proportion of their movements, so that all may easily hold their respective positions at the close of the dance.

There follows an interesting elaboration of the theory of the superexcellence of finely controlled moderation in all movement and gesture, with curious similies cited from Aristotle's philosophical discourses, wherein he praises the skill of the equilibrist, who knows how to keep the middle course, avoiding all extremes, and likewise applauds the art of the juggler, the minstrel and the ploughman.

Next we approach the technical side of the art of dancing, the pupil being informed that there are twelve movements used therein of which nine are natural and three accidental. The natural movements are to be performed on the accented beat (*il pieno*) and the three accidental ones on the off beat (*il vuodo*). 'And', he continues, 'the philosopher says that one cannot express the void [*il vuodo*]. I say that the void is silence and the fullness [*il pieno*] is speech. I say that the void is between one beat and the next, and that the fullness is instantly on the beat, thus making nine for thee as natural, while there are three for thee as accidental movements.'

The natural movements are declared as follows: '*scempio*[1] [single], *doppio* [double], *ripresa* [reprise], *continenza* [Italian version of the branle step], *reverenza* [reverence], *mezza volta* [half-circle], *volta tonda* [complete circle], *movimento* [elevation], *salto* [jump]: these being natural in themselves, since all can perform them independently of measure. The three accidentals are the following: *frappamento* [a flourish, or ornamental step], *scorsa* [rapid, gliding steps], and *cambiamento* [various forms of pirouette]. These three are acquired artificially, because they are not necessary according to nature.

'Note that the *doppio*, the *ripresa* and the *reverenza*, I declare to take 1 bar: the *scempio*, the *continenza*, the *mezzavolta*,[2] the *movimento* and the *salto* occupy half a bar: the *volta-tonda* consists of two bars. And this is according to the true movement of the *bassadanza*, measured in major imperfect time. In conclusion, the *frappamento*, *scorsa* and *cambiamento* are always a quarter bar, making one per bar and no more: and if you should, by mentality, be especially well adapted to this kind of virtuosity, you could put two into a bar; and thus juxtaposing two of them, they must always take one-eighth of a bar each. And while noting that the natural movements have each their order of measure and style, remember that these three that are acquired artificially, namely, *frappamento*, *scorsa* and *cambiamento*, are those which bring variety to the natural movements, and principally with the following: *scempio*, *doppio*, *ripresa* and *voltatonda*.[3] And note that the *frappamento* more than the others adapts itself, because, of all these four movements which are mentioned above as lending themselves to ornamentation, it assists in the performance of the *mezzavolta*: while, within the scope of a double, the *scorsa* can be employed. And though the *cambiamento* may not be generally suitable to the composition of a *bassadanza*, yet it may be seen in one of the following dances, named "la Corona"; but I affirm that it is never to be met with unless it be performed by some accomplished Master of the Art. And, except by such an one, this variety of ornament [*maniera*], which is very difficult is not made use of. Above all however let it be operated within the measure, of which measure I will give some explanation.

'Note that I now pray you to open your understanding, that you may comprehend what

[1] The spelling of this and the following names has been modernized.

[2] This appears to be a slip; other writers allot 1 bar to the half-circle and 2 to the whole circle.

[3] It should be understood that these added graces, termed 'accidental', are incorporated in the time measure of the basic step.

4

thing is measure of movement, this being the manner in which movements are composed upon the [rhythmic] measure. Measure in general, according to a tune or theme or movement, consists in measuring the alternation of the accented with the unaccented beat, measuring that of the silence with the hearing of the sound, measuring that of the movement of the body with the impact of the foot: otherwise it would not be possible to distinguish the beginning nor the middle nor the end of this action of dancing. And out of this general system of measure are differentiated four particular kinds. The first, which is slower than the others, is called by the name of Bassa Danza, in major[1] imperfect time. The 2nd measure is called Quadernaria, and is in minor imperfect time: which, by time measurement, is quicker than the Bassa Danza by one-sixth. The 3rd measure is called by the name of Saltarello, in major perfect time, that is to say, *passo brabante*; and this measure, by time measurement, is quicker than Quadernaria by another sixth, which amounts to one-third quicker than the Bassa Danza. The 4th and last measure is called by the common people, Piva and is in minor perfect time: This, in time measurement, abstracts from the Saltarello one-sixth. Thus this last measure named Piva, in minor perfect time arrives at being quicker than the Bassa Danza by three-sixths which constitutes one-half. These four measures govern the movement of the dancer and of the musician [*sonatore*], some slower and some faster. And herein is made manifest all the intellect and all the ignorance of the musicians, who will play the tune of a bassa danza and continually, from lack of understanding, accelerate the tempo from start to finish, and then will assert that they have performed a measure, talking nonsense; since they will in fact have made use of three. Because the beginning of the music will have been largo and have had the rhythm of major imperfect time; and you sonatore of small intelligence, always accelerating the tempo of the measure, in a short time will have arrived at that of the Quadernaria. You will hardly have plumbed the centre of the tune before you will have entered into the Saltarello. And this arises from the fact that the efficiency of the body is greater than that of the intellect, which intellect should act as a brake upon the hand. . . .

'And you, galante, now ask me what difference of mode exists between the bassa danza and the quadernaria as to the performance of the dance. I will tell you. Note that the bassa danza, which is in major imperfect time, begins its bar on the unaccented beat and completes it on the accented beat. Whereas the quadernaria, which is in minor imperfect, is the opposite, in that it begins its bar on the accented beat and completes it on the unaccented. Take note then, sonatore, when you begin to play a measure of bassa-danza, always commence the soprano [melody] before the beat of the tenore [ground], commencing it on the unaccented beat and the first note of the tenore should come on the accented beat. In the quadernaria, which is in minor imperfect time, you will do the contrary, namely you, sonatore, will always play the beat of the tenore and that of the soprano both together. I warn you that when you are playing the quadernaria, the beats of the tenore are more

---

[1] At this period duple time was classified as imperfect and represented by a half-circle, while a whole circle stood for triple or perfect time.

evenly spaced than those of the bassadanza, otherwise it would depart from its own style. But the Bassadanza, being slower [*piu larga*], as has already been said, you may place the beats of the tenore according to your pleasure provided that you keep the measure. And you, danzadore, note that when you commence a bassadanza you should always make a rising movement as you advance, so that the step may make the impact of the foot,[1] which [rising] movement will be made on the unaccented beat; and the step with the placing of the foot on the accented beat. And in the quadernaria it is the contrary, namely that you will begin with the step, by placing your foot: and this is the accented beat, and the other step which follows is on the unaccented. This is the difference between playing and dancing the bassadanza and the quadernaria.'

The master goes on to say that the saltarello is born of the bassadanza and commences its dancing bar on the off beat, whereas the piva, which is born of the quadernaria, begins its dancing bar on the accented beat, in common with the quadernaria. The respective speeds of these movements are once more explained at length, and then we arrive at one of the most interesting features of this treatise, that has always charmed me on account of its historical interest and the poetic fantasy of its exposition. This consists of a graded diagram of the rhythmic dance measures accompanied by individual descriptions in which each measure is made to speak for itself. Down the centre of the page are two vertical lines, divided by short horizontal ones into six equal parts. This device, to my thinking, bears some resemblance to an ancient method employed by the Chinese to determine their musical scale. To this end they constructed a series of mathematically proportioned tubes which, starting from C, produced, by a method of calculation based on rising fifths and descending octaves, a scale of C containing an F sharp as its fourth degree. Domenichino's tube-like diagram, proportioning the measure by sixths, intersects the written text, as can be seen in the adjoining translated version; and the description of each measure starts on a level with its appropriate dividing line.

This scale of measures has likewise something in common with the intricate system of musical rhythms, evolved by the Arabs from one original basic measure, corresponding with the walk of the camel. To this deliberate, measured pacing, which apparently never varied, the camel drivers of pre-Islamic times used to sing their songs as they escorted their caravans along the trade-routes to distant countries.

Thus the evolution of the dance measures of medieval Italy likewise evokes an impression of great antiquity for the serene and rhythmic pulsations of the 'Queen of Measures'.

A close study of the treatise of Domenichino and those of his successors reveals to us the surprising fact that early in the fifteenth century, amongst the vivacious Italian dancers, this formal dance had already diverged considerably from the classic French model as preserved in the dance-book of Marie de Bourgogne, thereby illustrating the natural adaptation of a dance to the character of its exponents.

[1] This rising movement is on the stationary foot, prior to making the impact of the stepping foot.

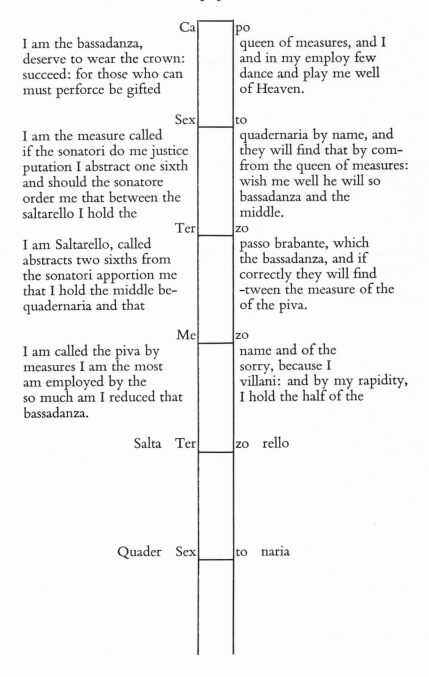

Ca | po

I am the bassadanza,   queen of measures, and I
deserve to wear the crown: and in my employ few
succeed: for those who can   dance and play me well
must perforce be gifted   of Heaven.

Sex | to

I am the measure called   quadernaria by name, and
if the sonatori do me justice   they will find that by com-
putation I abstract one sixth   from the queen of measures:
and should the sonatore   wish me well he will so
order me that between the   bassadanza and the
saltarello I hold the   middle.

Ter | zo

I am Saltarello, called   passo brabante, which
abstracts two sixths from   the bassadanza, and if
the sonatori apportion me   correctly they will find
that I hold the middle be-   -tween the measure of the
quadernaria and that   of the piva.

Me | zo

I am called the piva by   name and of the
measures I am the most   sorry, because I
am employed by the   villani: and by my rapidity,
so much am I reduced that   I hold the half of the
bassadanza.

Salta   Ter | zo   rello

Quader   Sex | to   naria

The remainder of the treatise consists of an elaborate analysis of the various modifications of tempo to which each of these dance measures may be subjected, and the necessity for the expert dancer to be able so to modify his pace and technique, in an impromptu manner, as to perform these measures (thus transformed) with a good grace. There is indeed a fine art in being able to adapt one's style and tempo so that the quick dances do not become clumsy nor the grave ones lose their dignity.

After these potential modifications of the measures have been fully dealt with, this abstract of Domenichino's treatise closes with the practical directions for the performance of fifteen *balli* with their music, and five *basse danze*, whose music is unfortunately omitted.

Assuming that 1416 was the date of the original treatise, of which remote date this surviving version bears the implication in the Roman characters heading the first page, and by the antique form of the dialect, we may conclude that Domenichino was born towards the close of the fourteenth century. From the fact that he is successively alluded to as 'da Piacenza' and as 'da Ferrara', by his pupils, Dr. Otto Kinkeldey concludes that he was a native of Piacenza, who in the course of time entered the service of the Marquess of Ferrara.[1] This conclusion is supported by internal evidence, as will appear from the following remarks.

The first two *balli* to be described in the performing section of this treatise bear the respective titles of 'Belriguardo' and 'Leoncello'. These titles suggest an approximate date for Domenichino's arrival at Ferrara, since 'Leonello' (a variant of 'Leoncello') was the name of the reigning Marquess of Ferrara from 1441 to 1450, while his magnificent country villa on the banks of the River Po was called 'Belriguardo'. Leonello was thirty-four when he succeeded his father, Niccolo; so it is possible that he had already been a pupil of Domenichino prior to his accession, and the *balli* in question may well have been composed in honour of this occasion.

It is strange that, although the successors of Domenichino furnish us with a large number of *basse danze* of his composition, this manuscript should contain only the aforementioned five, recorded in a small cramped hand, as though by an afterthought. Possibly the more ancient ones were already too well known to need further description and the scribe has therefore omitted them. Or, again, they might have been temporarily superseded at the court of Ferrara by the lighter and more varied *Balli*.

[1] A Jewish dancing-master of the Renaissance.

CHAPTER II

The Bassa Danza of the Renaissance

O F the two accredited pupils of Domenichino, namely, Guglielmo Ebreo and Antonio Cornazano, Guglielmo gives the more faithful rendering of the master's fundamental teaching with much additional matter of his own. His style, however, is more discursive than that of his teacher and, in place of his medieval simplicity, partakes of the full floridity of the Renaissance period.

The Guglielmo manuscripts in Sienna, Florence, and Paris show marked variations in detail and order of arrangement, the finest and most accurate being that in the Bibliothèque Nationale, Paris. This superb manuscript was made by the famous scribe Paganus Raudensis in 1463 for Francesco Sforza, fourth Duke of Milan, and is indeed an exquisite example of the art of the scribe, destined so soon to give place to that of the printer.

The preface and conclusion in this treatise provide interesting sidelights on the intellectual, artistic and musical gifts of the author, and on his exaggerated ideas of caste distinctions, where art and all the lofty conceptions of the mind are concerned. For him the *villani*, or peasants, are not only 'of the earth, earthy', but have corrupt minds.

Concerning music he says: 'Whatever the origin of the art may be, it is singularly worthy of admiration and praise, being indeed by no means least among the seven liberal arts, shewing itself to be lofty and sublime.'

Speaking of the concordance of four voices in the four principal kinds of composition, he continues: 'Which is of singular comfort to all our senses, almost as though it were the most natural sustenance of our spirits, albeit that there are in the world some people so inhuman as not to be moved with sublime pleasure by sweet melody and by the suave tones of concordant instruments ... without which no true happiness and perfection of living would be possible: as we ourselves frequently attest when, with so much assiduity, we foster in our houses charming and joyous little birds, so as to have from them the suave and dulcet fruit of their amorous and delightful songs, implanted by Nature in her

9

creatures: and which moreover often give to the infirm of spirit and the mentally afflicted the most exquisite joy. Which circumstance demonstrates the great excellence and supreme value of this science, whence the jocund art and sweet effect of the Dance has naturally proceeded. For this same virtue of the Dance is no other than the act of outward demonstration of the inward stirring of the spirit, which demonstration must accord with the measured and perfect consonances of this harmony.' After discoursing at some length on this subject, he explains with elaborate expressions of humility how he, the devoted disciple of the worthy cavalier 'Domenico of Ferrara', with a desire to render service and at the instance of many honest people, resolved to compile this treatise, assuring his readers that, if they study with attention the particulars contained therein and practise them carefully, then 'all will be able to dance in any festive surroundings with ease and security and much praise, and to exercise this virtuous art with confidence: Which, to all enamoured and generous hearts and gentle minds, led by divine inclination rather than through fortuitous talent, is most lovely and suitable; but is entirely alien and mortally inimical to depraved and mechanical plebeians, who at most times, with corrupted and perverse minds, make of a liberal art and virtuous science one that is impure and servile. ... To such as far as possible I deny it and trust that this work of mine may not come into their hands. But only to the honest and chaste, and to those who purely from desire will humbly adopt it with heartfelt affection, as a virtuous and joyous art, I recommend it and beg them to accept it with my good wishes.' Guglielmo closes his introductory chapter with further professions of humility and a willingness to submit to criticism on the part of his honoured preceptor or any other accomplished expert in the art.

In the succeeding chapter he takes us through the six qualifications necessary to a dancer, i.e. *Misura*, *Memoria*, *Partire di terreno*, *Aire*, *Maniera* and *Movimento corporeo*.

Concerning that of *Partire di terreno* (apportionment of the terrain), he says that there is need for much discretion and understanding of the right disposition of the dance, with an accurate appraisement of the evolutions to be performed in order that the dancers may come together without awkwardness or pause at the appointed beat, one kind of measurement being allowed for in a restricted aria and another in one that is wide and spacious.

The quality named *aire* he describes as an action of graceful rebound and resilience, the person exhibiting while dancing 'a sweet and human airiness'. 'It is needful', he continues, 'when one in dancing makes a single or a double or a reprise or a continenza or a gliding passeggio or a little jump [*saltarello*] to make an airy movement and to rise dexterously to the rhythmic beat; because, holding oneself down without rebound and airiness, would make the dance appear imperfect and unnatural; and it would seem to the assembled company to be lacking in grace and true excellence.'

The quality named *maniera* is explained as a sympathetic movement of the body in relation to that of the feet; so that, when the dancer performs a single or a double governed by the left foot, he turns the body leftwards, whereas he turns towards the right when such a step is governed by the right foot, maintaining it thus throughout the duration of the step.

Movimenti corporeo is explained as a supple alertness, such as can only exist in a healthy person.

Next we come to various rhythmic experiments in which the dancer should first make sure of keeping good time, and then obtain further rhythmic control by learning to dance contratempo or across the rhythm 'because' (maintains the author) 'one learns to recognize a thing and grasp it perfectly by trying its contrary'. There follow explanations of how the dancer may acquire complete control by dancing the opening bars of a *saltarello contratempo*, while the *sonatore* attempts to adapt his rhythm to that of the dancer and is constantly thwarted. On the other hand, the contrary experiment may be tried, in which the dancer keeps perfect time, while the *sonatore* endeavours to throw him out by distorting the rhythm, but is frustrated by the dancer.

These painful experiments concluded, we come to some interesting remarks on the subtle interpretation of the music by the dancer, who is told: 'Again, it must be noted that there are two modes, called minor and major, that he who would dance well a bassadanza or a saltarello or some other dance should learn to recognize.... And it is especially necessary that his steps and gestures be in accordance with these sweet voices: and the half-notes or the syncopations which are played in such and such a measure, whether in the minor or major, he should well understand and follow with his person and his gestures. And note that the major mode is more airy in its measure than is the minor, but is somewhat more harsh and less sweet.'

There are directions for one who would compose the music for a dance. Amongst other injunctions he is told that he may choose either a *tenore* (basic theme) or a tune, according to his fancy, 'which must be melodious and in perfect measure and should sound well ... and, above all, it must please the ladies'.

There are further recommendations concerning the need for great beauty and concordance in the music and the measure, which sweet concordance will charm the senses with a *suavissima dolcezza*, inspiring the dancers to sympathetic gesture and movement. To illustrate this point 'the miraculous effects of the sweet singing of marine monsters, as mentioned in classical literature' are cited; and it is stated that the emotions aroused in the onlookers by the sympathetic dancer 'are but the natural outcome of the inspiration he derives from the beauty of the music, without which the art of dancing would be sterile'.

For the young and virtuous lady, taking delight in the exercise of this art, certain rules are laid down. Firstly, it is stated that she needs to show more moderation and modesty than would a man. 'Her bearing should be gentle and suave, her bodily movement humble and affable, her deportment displaying a signorial dignity: and let her be light on her feet, with appropriate gesture: Her glances should not appear proud and roving, gazing here and there, as happens with many, but honest and for the most part lowered towards the ground: Not however, as some do, with her head sunk upon her breast, but carried high and responsive to the body, as though guided by the same natural movement, adroit, easy and controlled.'

This subject is further elaborated in the same vein, after which we arrive at book II, which consists of a series of arguments between master and pupil on all of the foregoing points in the author's system of teaching. Each objection or doubt raised by the pupil is logically refuted and demolished, thereby resolving his doubts and satisfying him as to all questions of established technique.

With some relief we then turn to the conclusion. Herein Guglielmo relates that it is thirty years since he first practised the science of dancing, and that during this time he has attended most of the solemn and noble court functions and festivals of Italy. The first two of these festive occasions which he mentions are (1) the entry into Milan of the most illustrious nobleman, Count Francesco Sforza, 'when his illustrious Signoria was created Duke, on his entry into this city' (1435) and (2) 'that of the most illustrious Marquess Leonello, that is, at his wedding in Ferrara' (1437). And thus he continues to enumerate these splendid ceremonies at which he has danced with distinction, 'not leaving aside those of the city of Venice and of the many other lords and gentlemen of Italy'.

He objects that at many of these festivals he has encountered certain presumptuous dancers who held themselves for masters, but who scarcely knew their right foot from their left; yet who thought that they could master the art and become experts in three days. He concludes by censuring all those who exercise the art improperly and exhorting such as would dance to do so worthily, observing the rules and precepts. 'And thus doing,' he assures them, 'you will be loved, honoured and revered everywhere: and of this enough.'

Hereupon our eyes are gratified with a charming miniature of three exquisite dancers performing a *bassa danza* to the music of a medieval harp, played by a seated harper. The date of this miniature appears, by the costumes, to be some years earlier than that of the treatise of Guglielmo.

In the Sienna and Florence manuscripts this little picture is mentioned but not reproduced. Both of these versions, moreover, describe it inaccurately as showing *two* dancers and one *sonatore*. From this we may deduce that the Paris manuscript (1463) is the earliest version of Guglielmo's treatise, although it omits all mention of Domenichino's scale of measures which is included in the Sienna manuscript, though in a mutilated form.

Antonio Cornazano, a native of Piacenza, was born in 1431, and would thus be the junior of Guglielmo by some fifteen or more years. We have from him one treatise, now in the Vatican Library. This is presumed to be a copy or second edition of an earlier one, now lost.[1] The original was composed for Ippolita Sforza, daughter of Francesco Sforza. Its dedicatory sonnet, bearing the date 1455, is repeated in the second edition, but is therein preceded by another in honour of 'Sforza Secondo', her half-brother.

Cornazano's treatise contains much interesting information of a practical nature in comparatively few words. He diverges slightly from Domenichino and Guglielmo in

[1] Otto Kinkeldey, op. cit.

certain technical details and terminology, though agreeing with them on all points of fundamental importance. This is a natural occurrence in the plastic art of dancing, wherein each great exponent may leave the impress of his own interpretation, although adhering to the essential structure of the Dance.

He enumerates in his opening discourse six requisite qualities for the dancer, namely: *Memoria, Misura, Maniera, Aere, Diversita di cose* (in place of Guglielmo's *Movimento corporeo*), and lastly *Compartimento di terreno* (equivalent of Guglielmo's *partire del terreno*). *Diversita di cose* is explained as the art of diversifying a step as a means of expression, thus avoiding a mechanical dullness. Much stress is laid upon the need for airy lightness on the part of the lady, and 'Madonna Beatrice' (sister of Duke Borso[1] of Ferrara) is instanced as pre-eminent in this respect, when leading the dance as queen of the festival; so that none who would imitate her example could do aught amiss. 'And in order to inspire you to emulate her lightness,' he concludes, 'I will quote a Ferrarese proverb, which is this: Who would be transported from this World to the Beyond, must listen to the playing of Pierobono: Who would find the Heavens opened, must experience the liberality of Duke Borso.[2] Who would see the Earthly Paradise, let him watch Madonna Beatrice[3] reigning over the Feast.'

Here follows a most enlightening definition of the steps appropriate to each dance:

'Piva consists of naught else than double paces animated and accelerated by the rapidity of the measure, and which the balladore himself dances in spirited fashion. Saltarello is the gayest of all dances, and the Spanish call it Alta Danza: it consists only of double paces, undulated by the elevation on the short second step which divides the first and second bars [i.e. the musical bars in triple time, of which two compose the dancing bar] and is swayed outwards by the springing movement accompanying the first step, which is made by the body, as before explained.

'Quadernaria is, properly speaking, the German Saltarello, which consists of two single paces and one ornamented reprise, beaten behind the second step crossways [*ripresetta battuta dietro il secondo passo in traverso*].

'Bassa Danza is queen of the other measures and should be adorned with all the six qualities above described, in the definition of the art of dancing.'

Hereupon Cornazano gives an outline of the system of measures developed from and enchained with one another. He however reverses their order, making the *Piva* or *Cornamusa* the starting-point, because, he asserts, this is the lowest grade in the scale of measures, being as a stream from which the others branch off. He continues: 'Among our practitioners it used to be the principal kind of music for high dancing; but at the present time, having been minced up by the ingenious ones into more florid movements, it has become low and vulgar and unsuitable for magnificent persons and dancers of good standing. Yet if, in spite of this, one should come to dance it, it is not fitting for the lady otherwise than

[1] Created duke in 1450.   [2] Brother of Leonello and reigning duke of Ferrara 1450–71.
[3] Later became the wife of Niccoló da Correggio.

in its natural steps; and in order to assist the man in his turns according to the pirouettes and high jumps that he may choose to make, both straight and in reverse and revolving inwards or outwards; it is requisite that she should be alert and well skilled therein for maintaining the measure, which is worth more than the other.

'In the Saltarello, its natural steps should be supple with swayings and undulations, according to the mode previously described. It is becoming to the lady to mingle therewith some pleasing graces, such as two single paces in one bar, swayed and undulated, and sometimes three contrapassi in two bars; and these two things may follow one another. And, let him differ who will, the lady should never include in her bar a high leap, nor the man either, except very occasionally, if he be a skilled dancer.

'The Quadernaria measure is not used by itself as a dance among the Italians, but when introduced into a Ballo[1] serves to embellish it, as is the case with "la Sobria" where the men change places and come behind the lady: And similarly in "la Prisonera", where the man and the lady take hold of each other.

'In the Bassa Danza, the steps of which it is composed should be made with supple, swaying movements and undulations. It is not beautiful if the reprises and the continenzas be not differentiated the one from the other: that is, made large or very small respectively; and after the one that is large the other is never made the same, and thus they form a contrast. Sometimes it is not ill looking to remain motionless with suspended animation for the space of a bar, then to enter into the following bar with airy vivacity like a person restored from death to life. In this, Messer Domenichino, your good servant and my master, has shown superlative judgement, pronouncing the dancing of a grave measure in particular to be similar to a whimsical flight of fancy [*ombra phantasmatica*], by which simile and expression many things are understood which can not be explained otherwise.

'Let them be admonished therefore, these masters of acrobatics and mincing feet, that this subtle grace is signorial, and that if it were to be omitted, then would the Bassa Danza degenerate into mere commonplace movements and lose the essential attributes of its true nature.

'The Dance contains within itself nine natural, bodily movements and three accidental. The natural are singles, doubles, reprises,[2] continenzas, counterpaces [*contrapassi*], high-jumps [*movimenti*], whole circles, half-circles, and revolving turns [*scambi*]. *The accidentals* are scurrying steps [*trascorse*], flourishes [*frappamenti*], and diminutions [*pizzighamenti*]. And none of these is suitable for a [lady][3] excepting however the diminutions.'

Here follows a reiteration of the steps suitable to the four types of dances. The *Piva* employs only the double, performed *prestissimo*. The *Saltarello* uses singles and reprises when combined with a *bassa danza*, and also doubles and counterpaces when danced to its full extent: i.e. as an independent dance. The *Quadernaria* adapts itself to the type of *ballo* into which it is introduced.

[1] A suite of dance movements.   [2] English form of the Italian *ripresa*.
[3] Word missing.

The Bassa Danza of the Renaissance

In the *Bassa Danza*, all of the nine natural steps may be introduced, excepting only the *movimento*. This name is applied by Cornazano to the high jump (the step which essentially differentiates a *bassa* from an *alta danza*). The action of rising on the toes prior to stepping, to which the name of *movimento* is applied by Domenichino, is called by Cornazano *alzamento*, or as we might say 'elevation'. But the jump may be introduced possibly in *balletti*. The man, when dancing with a lady in public, is allowed to bestow upon her an *honestissimo* glance of tender solicitude. 'And all these things', continues Cornazano, 'are "bellissima" for the lady in every measure of the dance, provided that she goes with swaying and undulating movements of the body in the manner described.

'The three accidental movements, as they are not required to adorn the dancing of the lady, I will not further define: let it suffice to have specified them; and besides the style of their vocabulary is sufficient for any dancer.

'The Balletti are a composition of diverse measures which may contain in themselves all the nine natural bodily movements, arranged each one with some fundamental appropriateness, as will appear from that of "la Mercancia" and that of "la Sobria", which are contrary in sentiment the one to the other.' He speaks of the need for an excellent memory in the dancing of these *balletti*, and claims that, having on certain occasions seen a new *ballo* or a *bassa danza* performed but once in some signorial salon, he was forthwith able to join in the said dance and go through with it without a single error.

Here follows the timing of the steps:

> 2 singles—1 bar
> 1 double—1 bar
> 1 reprise—1 bar
> 2 continenzas—1 bar
> 3 counterpaces—2 bars
> 1 half-circle—1 bar
> 1 whole circle—2 bars
> The pirouettes—1 bar or nothing
> The jumps: are not regular
> The accidentals: are according to pleasure

It is here pointed out that there is a kind of measure, apart from the musical measure, which consists of a well-judged vivacity in the rising movement of an undulation.

The undulation is none other than a slow raising of the whole person and a rapid sinking.

'Of all the things that are danced besides the balletti by us Italians in distinguished salons, the most frequently used are the Saltarello and the Bassa Danza: and the Saltarello, as has been said, is called by the Spaniards "Alta Danza" and consists of the passo brabante: and it is derived from the Bassa Danza, since it is always performed after it.

'With the Bassa Danza each bar is divided into four parts: the off beat is one, that is to say, the first movement: emerging from this are the 3 steps which occupy each one a quarter-bar, that which constitutes the off beat and the three other quarters. But this can be best explained by seeing it done.'

Here follows Cornazano's exposition of the gradation of the measures, these being, he maintains, originally all derived from the basic *Piva*. It is accompanied by his diagram of a ladder whose lowest rung is allotted to the *Piva*. This, he explains, is of low or rustic origin; and was formerly played by shepherds on pan-pipes. By ascending the ladder, whose rungs widen in correct mathematical proportion through the scale of measures, one attains to the *Bassa Danza*, which crowns the summit. Thus he arrives, by tortuous reasoning, at a reversal of Domenichino's theory of the derivation of the measures from the *Bassa Danza*, the *Queen of Measures*.

The subject of the potential modifications of the measures is exhaustively elaborated, apparently with a view to establishing their fundamental proportions (as with Guglielmo) by experimenting on the effects of adapting them to alien rhythms and tempi, this experience being supposed to endow the dancer with complete mastery of the rhythmic art.

'Let us now', he concludes, 'come to certain Balli and Basse Danze which stand apart from the common dances and have been fashioned for signorial halls, and only to be danced by stately ladies and not by plebeians.'

There follow seven *balli* with their music and some *basse danze* without their music, and, finally, the music of three tenore for *basse danze*, said to be among the most famous. These however do not bear the names of any of the foregoing dances, but are entitled respectively:

> *Tenore del Re di Spagna*
> *Canzon de pisari dicto la Ferrarese*
> *Tenore Colinetto.*

In the Paris Bibliothèque Nationale there is a beautiful manuscript which purports to be a treatise by a dancing-master named Giovanni Ambrogio (Fonds it. 476). It is in actual fact a literal replica of the Paris treatise of Guglielmo (Fonds it. 973), both as to title[1] and text (except for a few inaccuracies). At the end, however, there are some additional paragraphs concerning the style of dancing suitable to various types of costume, and a closing chapter in which Ambrogio (despite the fact that he has already arrogated to himself all of Guglielmo's personal experiences at the festivals in the ducal courts of Italy)[2] describes the sumptuous court functions at which he has apparently really been present. Herein, I regret to say, he enlarges solely on the subject of the magnificent viands, such as roasted peacocks and confections of marzipan and sugar, which have graced these splendid feasts; and his literary style has none of the elegance and poetic feeling of that of Guglielmo. The fact that he attaches his own name to the dances composed by Guglielmo

---

[1] *De pratica seu arte tripudii vulgare opusculum*, his own name being substituted for that of Guglielmo.

[2] These include marriage feasts held in Milan, Ferrara, Pesaro, Urbino, Bologna and Venice.

(respecting only the acknowledged authorship of those ascribed to Domenichino) suggests the hypothesis that he was Guglielmo's successor at one or another of the ducal courts and stepped most thoroughly into his predecessor's shoes.

This theory gains some support from an anecdote, recounted by Dr. A. Luzzio in his book entitled *I Precettori d'Isabella d'Este*. Herein he mentions that when Isabella (aged six) was newly affianced to Francesco Gonzaga (future Marquess of Mantua), special envoys were sent to Ferrara to report upon her charms. One of these informed the Marquess Federico Gonzaga that he had seen the young Madonna dance with her master, Messer Ambrogio, a Jew in the service of the Duke of Urbino, and that she exhibited a grace and beauty of movement quite astonishing in one so young. Since Isabella d'Este was born in 1474, this would place the date of this occurrence as 1480, about seventeen years after the time when Guglielmo's great treatise was issued.

We have no further records of the *Bassa Danza* and *Saltarello* until we arrive at the date of Caroso's treatise *Il Ballarino*, published in 1581, which professes to give us the most famous dances of France, Spain and Italy; and which, although published at this late date, is certainly retrospective, since Caroso is reputed to have been born *c.* 1527.

His portrait forming the frontispiece to his 1581 treatise gives his age as 46; but the same portrait, reproduced in *Nobilita dei Dame* (1600), gives it as 73, confirming 1527 as birth-date.

The name of the *Bassa Danza* has been shortened by Caroso to *Bassa* and one of the examples given is named 'Bassa e Alta', a dance cited in Caroso's later treatise[1] as being of Spanish origin.

[1] *Nobilita dei Dame.*

CHAPTER III

How to Dance the Bassa Danza of Spain and Italy

OUR desire now is to realize a *bassa danza* of the period when Domenichino compiled his interesting treatise. This takes us back to the dawn of the fifteenth century. Here we are faced with an initial difficulty, arising from the fact that in the one surviving copy of this treatise, although the style and technique of the 'Queen of Measures' is treated of in some detail, no music for an entire *bassa danza* is supplied. Neither is there any formula therein for these earlier dances; whereas many of the later *balli* dating from *c.* 1440 onwards, which contain short sections of *bassa danza*, interspersed with other dance movements, are well explained and accompanied by their music. The treatise closes with three later *basse danze* whose description is written in a cramped and almost illegible hand which suggests that they are a later addition. They include such unusual features as the *salto* and the *scambiamento*, which steps Domenichino has declared to be inappropriate to the *Bassa Danza*.

Happily Guglielmo atones for this lack.

In his Sienna manuscript he retails the formulae for twenty-four *basse danze* by Domenichino and six others by himself. Here we have plenty from which to choose, as regards the dances, but still no music!

This difficulty can however be surmounted in the case of two typical examples, the first of which is ascribed to Domenichino, while the second, entitled *Venus*, from the Magliabechiana manuscript, is ascribed therein to Lorenzo de Medici.

Domenichino's dance is named *La Spagna*. It is for two dancers, hand in hand; and the character of its steps is consistent with the earliest type of *bassa danza*, serene and spacious. For accompanying music, I find that the popular tenore, *El Re di Spagna* (preserved for us by Cornazano), when provided with a descant and a middle part, is entirely appropriate, only requiring the repeat of the last phrase to agree with the measure of the dance.

Before describing the movements of this dance I will illustrate the natural positions

18

of the feet when stationary, so as to simplify all technical instructions throughout this book.

The steps should be *very small*.

The Positions

1st	♭♂	Position		
2nd	♭ ♂	Position		
3rd	♭♂	right	♂♭	left
4th	♭ ♂	right	♭ ♂	left
5th	♭	right	♂	left

The Italian *Bassa Danza* is not restricted to two dancers or to two or more couples dancing independently, as was usual in other countries. We learn from the Italian treatises that the number of dancers ranged from two to three, four, six or eight *alla fila*. The earliest examples favour two or three dancers, and in the latter case they may consist of two ladies and one man, or of two men and one lady.

In the Italian *Bassa Danza* the partners use identical feet, unless instructed otherwise. When holding hands, they do so lightly, by the finger-tips. In some early illustrations they are shown with the little fingers hooked.

Although the opening and closing reverence of salutation are not included in the formula for *La Spagna*, they should nevertheless be performed, but outside of the music. To this end I have introduced a chord in arpeggio at the beginning and end of the tune.

19

LA SPAGNA

The order of the steps

(Reverence)	
2 continenzas l.r.	1 bar
2 singles r.l.	1 bar
4 doubles r.l. (alternately)	4 bars
1 reprise r.	1 bar
2 singles l.r.	1 bar
2 doubles l.r.	2 bars
2 reprises l.r.	2 bars
2 singles l.r.	1 bar
1 double l.	1 bar
1 double in retreat r.	1 bar
1 reprise (revolving) l.	1 bar
1 reprise (sideways) r.	1 bar
(Reverence)	

HOW TO PERFORM THE STEPS

The partners face forward, hand in hand, but turned obliquely towards each other.

Reverence: On the first beat, stand erect with the weight resting on the right foot, and with the left advanced so that the heel is level with the middle of the right foot and four inches apart. This coincides with what is called the fourth position left. On the second beat, draw back the left foot so that the toe is level with the right heel and the foot flat on the ground, whilst inclining the head and shoulders. On the third beat, transfer the weight to the left foot, bending both knees outwards: at the half-beat, straighten the right knee (still keeping both feet on the ground). On the fourth beat, transfer the weight forward on to the right foot, rising on the toes, and join the left foot to it in the first position, standing once more erect.

Flat-heeled shoes with flexible soles should be worn, thus allowing the movement of ankle and instep to be entirely supple. The partners use identical feet throughout.

The continenzas, left and right: On the first beat, rising on the toes, step sideways with the left foot, about four inches distant from the right; and at the same time sway the left hip outwards slightly, keeping the toes of both feet on the ground: at the half-beat, sink on to the flat on the left foot, inclining the head towards the right. On the second beat, join the right foot to the left in the third position right, bending both knees outwards: at the half-beat, rise on the toes with straightened knees and head erect. On the third and fourth beats, perform the right continenza in similar fashion, stepping towards the right. The continenzas are the Italian version of the *branle* step used in the French *Bassesdanses*.

THREE MEDIEVAL DANCERS

Arm movements: These should be moderate and gracefully curved, serving to emphasize the rhythm and to produce an effect of co-ordinated movement. They are a part of the *maniera*. The upper arm should remain lowered but free, and sometimes the rhythmic emphasis may be confined to slight turns of hand and wrist. To grace the reverence, let the free arm, during the first and second beats, be drawn inward at elbow level with the hand raised, as represented in the miniature of three medieval dancers. On the third beat, lower the arm with an outward curving motion, and on the fourth beat draw it slightly inward and upward again. In the continenzas a gentle outward and inward movement terminated by the raising of the hand accords well with each sideways step.

The singles: The instructions for *La Spagna* indicate that the first pair of singles begins with the right foot; but the second and third pair, occurring later in the dance, are directed to begin with the left. For the right single: On the first beat, step forward on the flat of the right foot, and sway the body outwards with graceful flexibility: on the second beat, rise on the toes. On the third and fourth beats, perform the left single in similar fashion, using the left foot, and swaying towards the left. It produces a pleasing effect to turn the head somewhat in the opposite direction from that towards which the body leans, and to allow the free hand to balance the movements of the body with a graceful sideways motion.

The doubles: The first group of doubles in *La Spagna* also begins with the right foot. On the first beat, step forward lightly with the right foot on the tip of the toes. On the second beat, step forward with the left, also on the toes. On the third beat, step again with the right, but this time on the flat of the foot, and sway the body outwards to the right with suavity. On the fourth beat, rise on the toes. The left double is made in similar fashion, starting with the left foot.

If you should desire to produce the soaring effect extolled by Domenichino as *fantasmata* (wherein the dancer pauses immobile on the third step of the double and then suddenly 'takes wing like the falcon'), proceed as follows: Having made the first 2 steps of the double on the first and second beats of the bar, on the third, step on the flat of the foot, bending the knee of the stationary foot a little as you step, but straightening it as you land. Then pause until near the close of the fourth beat, when you rise swiftly on to the toes, and (with an airy gesture of the free hand and arm outward and upward) arrive promptly on the first beat of the succeeding bar, with the first step of the following double. This must be made as before, daintily on tiptoe and with well-straightened knees. This kind of *maniera* demands an easy grace and a good sense of proportion. If this cannot be achieved naturally, the dancer will nevertheless produce a good effect, though adhering strictly to the beat, if the steps are performed with a supple undulation.

The reprise: The first reprise in *La Spagna* comes singly. It begins with the right foot and is made in retreat. On the first beat (facing front, but turning the body a little towards the right), step backwards with the right foot, flat on the ground, and with the knee slightly bent. On the second beat, draw back the left foot to join the right in the third position left, rising on the toes with well-straightened knees. On the third and fourth beats, repeat the same movements, stepping back with the right foot and joining the left foot to it in the third position left, rising on the toes. The backward step should be rather larger than the steps of the singles and doubles (which approximate four inches).

The pair of reprises which occur in the middle of the dance should be done sideways to left and right, thus: After the preceding pair of doubles (l.r.), let the man make a quarter-turn *right* on his right foot, and the lady a quarter-turn *left* on her right foot. Thus the two partners will be facing each other but turned sideways to the spectators, and will consequently move in contrary motion. The pair of reprises will occupy 2 bars. On the first beat of bar one, step sideways on the flat of the left foot with slightly bent knee. On the second beat, join the right foot to the left in the third position right, rising on the toes. On the third and fourth beats, repeat these movements, still stepping leftwards. The second reprise will be made towards the right, stepping with the right foot and joining up the left, in the third position left. As the partners will have been moving in contrary directions, they will be once more level with one another at the close of the second reprise. At this point the man makes a quarter-turn *left* on his right foot, and the lady a quarter-turn *right* on her right foot. They will now be facing the onlookers again. Throughout these 2 reprises the man holds the lady's right hand in his own; but when they resume their normal positions facing forward, he will once more take her left hand in his right, as they advance with the ensuing pair of singles.

The last pair of doubles differs from the previous ones in that, although the first double (l.) advances as before, the second one (r.) is made stepping backwards.

The dance closes with a pair of reprises (l.r.), the first of which is made revolving in lively style (*in volta alla gioiosa*) and the second one in retreat. For the first, let go hands, and on the first beat, place the left foot (flat) in front of the right in the fifth position left, bending both knees outwards. On the second beat, rising on the toes, make a half-turn right. On the third beat, place the left foot (whose position has been reversed by the half-turn), once more, in front of the right in the fifth position left, bending the knees. On the fourth beat, rising on the toes, make another half-turn right, which will bring you back into your original position facing forward. For the second reprise, take hands again (the man taking the lady's left hand in his right) and make a right reprise in retreat in the same manner as the first reprise (r.) which follows the four doubles at the beginning of the dance.

On the closing chord, in arpeggio, make a reverence similar to that which opens the dance. Although the dancers are facing forward for the reverence they should turn their heads towards one another at the close.

It will be remembered that Domenichino reckons the composite steps of the Italian *Bassa Danza* from the fourth beat of the preceding bar (*il vuodo*), which is marked by an elevation, to the third beat of the bar proper (*il pieno*), which is marked by a step. For practical purposes, however, I have followed the system of all other writers in describing the actual movements as they take place within the musical bar. This in no way affects the technical procedure, since Domenichino's subdivision of the composite steps serves merely as a theoretical differentiation between the fluent *Bassa Danza* and the four-square quadernaria [apparently the parent, jointly, of the *Allemande* and the *Paduana* (otherwise *Pavana*)]. Domenichino likened the alternate elevation and sinking of the steps in a *bassa danza* to the rise and fall of a gondola on the wavelets of a tranquil sea.

LA SPAGNA

23

double   double

reprise   reprise

2 singles   double

double   reprise

reprise   congé

VENUS TU MA PRIS

The next example I would like to bring to your notice is the *Bassa Danza Venus* for three dancers, consisting of one man and two ladies.

This dance is attributed to Lorenzo de Medici in the Florentine version of Guglielmo's treatise, wherein it is set forth in detail.[1] In the Sienna manuscript we find its name included among a list of dances ascribed to Domenichino[2]: but this might be an earlier version and no description is appended. The gay figures of the *Gioioso* may well have been added by the illustrious prince Lorenzo de Medici and form a pleasing contrast to the formal opening movement.

The title *Venus* is not the Italian name for the goddess, which would be *Venere*; and we may therefore conclude that the music for this dance was derived from a French popular song. In a collection of instrumental arrangements of fifteenth-century French popular songs, first published in Venice in 1501, under the title, *Harmonice Musices Odhecaton*, there occurs one, entitled *Venus tu ma* [sic] *pris*. This I assume to have been based on the original song to which this *bassa danza* was composed; the more so as the music fits the dance perfectly.

THE FIGURES OF BASSA DANZA VENUS

Opening movement: Section 1: The three dancers stand in a row, with the man between the two ladies. In the description of the various evolutions, the lady on the man's right will be called *first lady*, and the other on his left, *second lady*. During the first bar the dancers, holding hands and facing the assembled company, make a slow continenza (*continenza grave*), which occupies the whole 4 beats. In the second bar they advance with 2 singles (l.r.), at the close of which they separate, the man making a quick half-turn left on his right foot, so that he has his back to the spectators. During the third and fourth bars he makes 2 oblique sideways reprises (l.r.), retreating in zigzag fashion while the ladies continue to advance with 2 doubles (l.r.) facing forward.

Opening movement: Section 2: All three make a left half-turn on the right foot, so as to form a triangle with the man now facing forward (at the foot of the dance) and the ladies turned towards him, with their backs to the onlookers. In the first and second bars, all three make 2 sideways reprises (l.r.). In the third bar, they approach one another with a left double; and in the fourth bar, while the man advances with 2 singles l.r. to take his place between the two ladies, they make a reverence to him.

[1] Magliabechiana. Class XIX. 9. 88.
[2] Communal Library, Sienna, L. V. 29.

How to Dance the Bassa Danza of Spain and Italy

THE FIGURES OF THE GIOIOSO

Figure I: Section 1: The man turns towards the first lady and takes her right hand in his own, holding it shoulder high. In the first and second bars, they revolve to the right with 2 gioioso doubles (l.r.). Releasing her hand, he turns toward the second lady and takes her left hand in his own while they revolve to the left during the third and fourth bars with 2 gioioso doubles (r.l.).

Figure I: Section 2: The three dancers take hands, facing forward. In the first and second bars, they perform 2 sideways reprises (moving to left and right), and during the third and fourth bars, all three make a slow reverence. The man, who retains his hold of one hand of each lady, should step back a pace on his right foot instead of advancing the left; and the ladies, advancing the left foot, should turn slightly in his direction.

Figure II: Section 1: All three dancers face forward but without holding hands. In the first and second bars, the man advances with 2 gioioso doubles, while the two ladies make sideways reprises in opposite directions, the first lady making 2 to the right, and the second lady 2 to the left. At the close of the second bar, the man makes a rapid half-turn left on his right foot so as to be with his back to the spectators and facing the ladies; during the third and fourth bars, he makes 2 sideways reprises (l.r.). Meanwhile the ladies, who have widened the distance between themselves, close in again with 2 sideways reprises, the first lady making 2 to the left and the second lady 2 to the right.

Figure II: Section 2: This section opens with 2 bars of saltarello steps for all three, by means of which the two ladies advance, while the man approaches them, passing between them. At the close of this manœuvre he makes a rapid half-turn left on his right foot so as to face forward; while the ladies, who have passed a little way beyond him, also make a half-turn left on their right foot, so as to face him. During the third and fourth bars all three make a slow reverence, at whose close each lady, advancing the right foot, makes a rapid half-turn left on it, so as to face forward and be in line with the man, who comes between them again.

Figure III: Section 1: All three face forward, holding hands. In the first and second bars, they make 2 sideways reprises (l.r.). In the third bar, the two ladies make 2 sideways gioioso singles, while the man, stepping forward with his first single, turns a half-turn, left on the second, so as to face them. In the fourth bar, all three make a short reverence (*mezza riverenza*), at the close of which the man makes a rapid half-turn left, on his right foot, so as to place himself once more between the two ladies.

Figure III: Section 2: The three dancers face forward and, hand in hand, make 2 sideways reprises (l.r.) during the first and second bars. In the third and fourth bars they make a slow, ceremonial reverence towards the assembled company. This closes the dance: but the dancers are directed to perform it a second time.

HOW TO PERFORM THE STEPS OF BASSA DANZA VENUS

Opening movement: Section 1

The dance opens with a slow continenza called *continenza grave*. Facing the company, the dancers stand in a row holding hands lightly by the finger-tips. On the first beat, rising on the toes with well-straightened knees, they step sideways on the left foot. On the second beat, transferring the weight entirely to the left foot, they sink on to the flat of the foot. On the third beat, they join the right foot to the left in the third position right, bending the knees outwards and inclining the head gently. On the fourth beat, they rise on the toes and raise the head again.

The pair of singles. On the first beat, still holding hands, all three step forward on the flat of the left foot with slightly bent knees. On the second beat, they rise on the toes, swaying the body towards the left. This is the left single. During the third and fourth beats, the right single is made in similar fashion, but stepping with the right foot and with the body swaying to the right. The dancers release hands and the man instantly makes a rapid half-turn left on his right foot, so as to face backward.

Sideways reprises: These are made to left and right across the *stage* (I use this term for convenience). On the first beat, the man steps sideways on the flat of the left foot, bending the knees a little and raising the left hip. On the second beat, with a sliding movement he joins the right foot to the left in the first position, rising on the toes. On the third beat, he steps again sideways on the flat of the left foot, with bent knees, and on the fourth beat, he slides the right foot to join the left in the first position, rising on the toes. The right reprise is made in similar fashion, stepping with the right foot and moving towards the right. In this particular instance it would facilitate the evolution of the three dancers if the man proceeds with a slightly zigzag motion, by turning obliquely (but very little so) leftwards during the left reprise and to the right during the right reprise. By this small bias towards the one hand or the other, he will help to increase the distance between himself and the two ladies, making a semi-retreat, that will be helpful in the ensuing foregathering of the dancers.

Whilst the man is making these 2 reprises, the ladies advance to the head of the dance with 2 doubles (l.r.), which are made as follows:

The doubles: On the first beat (of the third bar), the two ladies advance in open formation, stepping lightly on the toe of the left foot, with straightened knees. On the second beat, they make another little step on the right toe. On the third beat, they again step with the left foot, but this time on the flat of the foot, bending the knee and swaying to the left. On the fourth beat, they make the elevation, rising on the toes, to prepare the way for the right double. This will be made in similar fashion, using reverse feet and swaying towards the right. At the close of the second double, both ladies make a half-turn left on the right foot and thus face backward, opposite to the man.

Opening movement: Section 2

Sideways reprises: These are made to left and right and are as described in section 1, except that there is no zigzag progress, the dancers moving exactly crossways.

The double and singles. The left double and the pair of singles are performed as described in section 1. To allow enough room for the ladies to make their reverence towards him, the man may, if necessary, slant his singles a little sideways.

The reverence: This is a ceremonial salutation made by the two ladies as the man approaches them. On the first beat, they advance the left foot about four inches, with the weight resting on the right foot. On the second beat, they draw the left foot back a few inches behind the right heel, inclining the head and body. On the third beat, after bending the knees outwards they transfer the weight to the left foot, straightening the right knee. On the fourth beat, restoring the weight forward to the right foot, they join up the left foot in the first position, rising on the toes and straightening the head and body: they then sink the heels at the close.

HOW TO PERFORM THE STEPS OF THE GIOIOSO

Figure I: Section 1

The gioioso double: Each double occupies 1 bar, composed of 6 beats, and is therefore spaced unevenly. It should be performed airily with graceful undulation. For the left double: On the first beat, step forward lightly on the toe of the left foot, remaining thus during the second beat. On the third beat, step forward on the right toe in the same manner. On the fourth beat, step forward with the left foot, but this time with the flat of the foot, bending the knee and swaying gently towards the left, while turning the head a little to the right. During the fifth beat, bring up the right foot behind the left heel, rising on the toes. On the sixth beat, sink the left heel.

For the right double follow the same procedure, stepping first with the right foot.

Section 2

The sideways reprise: This should be the diminished reprise, called by the Italians *ripresa minuita*, especially appropriate to this gay movement of the dance. The sideways travelling of this kind of reprise is motivated by means of the alternate opening and closing of heels and toes, through the sideways movement of the heel of one foot and the toe of the other. At the start, stand with feet joined in the first position, heels together and toes apart. To travel leftwards, move the left heel and the right toe in that direction, producing thereby the first *false* position, with the toes joined and the heels apart. Next move leftwards the left toe and the right heel. This restores the feet to the normal first position, but removed some inches towards the left. This manoeuvre constitutes a double twist. Theoretically, one double twist goes to a beat, but, as the dancer acquires fluency

28

he ceases to count the movements and, by making them smaller and quicker, produces a rippling effect which is delightful to the onlooker. The movement should finish with the feet joined in the first position. Carry the head erect and make no movement of shoulders or hips, but appear to sail along without effort.

The slow reverence: This will occupy 2 bars of 6 beats. On the first beat of bar one, advance the left foot about four inches with the weight resting on the right foot: at the half-bar, draw back the left foot a few inches behind the right heel, inclining the head and body. On the first beat of the second bar, bend the knees outwards and transfer the weight on to the left foot, thereby straightening the right knee: at the half-bar, restoring the weight to the right foot, join the left to it in the first position and rise on the toes, straightening the head and body. At the close of the bar, sink the heels. This concludes the second section of figure I of the *gioioso* movement.

STEPS OF THE GIOIOSO

Figure II: Section 1

The doubles and sideways reprises which compose this section should be performed as in figure 1 of this gioioso movement.

Figure II: Section 2

Saltarello step: In the fifteenth century this graceful, lilting step was named the *pas de Brabant.* It was a composite step occupying 1 bar of 6 beats, and would be performed alternately to left and right. On the first beat, step forward on the flat of the left foot, and on the second beat, rise on the toes. On the third beat, join up the right foot behind the heel of the left, still remaining on the toes. On the fourth beat, step again, on the *flat* of the left foot, and during the fifth beat, rise on to the ball of the foot. On the sixth beat, hop lightly on the left foot and simultaneously raise the right foot forward a few inches from the ground with pointed toe. This step should be enhanced by airy sideways movements of hand and forearm. In the following bar, step with the right foot, making the same series of movements. This completes our 2 bars of saltarello steps.

The slow reverence: This will occupy 2 bars of 6 beats and should be performed as described in the second section of figure I of this movement.

The arm movements: These are a very important adjunct to this ornate ceremonial salutation. During the first bar, draw the left hand and forearm inward and upward with a curved movement and, during the second bar, downward and outward with a graceful sweeping gesture.

Figure III: Section 1

The reprises: The sideways reprises which open this figure should be performed as described in figure I of this gioioso movement.

The gioioso singles: These take half a bar each and usually go in pairs. The man, in this instance, steps forward and turns at the close. On the first beat, step forward on the flat of the left foot, with slightly bent knee and swaying the body a little towards the left. On the second beat, join up the right foot behind the left, just touching the heel and rising on the toes. On the third beat, sink the left heel. This completes the left single, which is followed by the right single at the second half of the bar, stepping with the right foot and following the same procedure, except that during the fifth beat, while rising on the toes a half-turn left is made before sinking the right heel on the sixth beat. The dancer thus closes his pair of singles in the fifth position, left with the weight resting on the right foot.

The two ladies make their singles *sideways* instead of forwards; otherwise the movements are the same. The first lady makes her first single to the right and her second single to the left, while the second lady makes hers to left and right. They thus open and close the space between them, taking care to leave enough room for the man to resume his position between them after the short reverence which closes this section. A slight movement of head and hands in the opposite direction from the body movement enhances the singles.

The short reverence: This is a passing salutation, performed in two movements, and occupying 1 bar of 6 beats. On the first beat, draw back the left foot a few inches behind the right, at the same time bending both knees outwards and making a moderate inclination of head and body. At the half-bar, restore the left foot beside the right in the first position, rising on the toes with knees straight and head and body once more erect. On the sixth beat, sink the heels. The man (who has his back to the spectators for this short reverence), after making his inclination in the first half of the bar, then joins his left foot to the right on the fourth beat, but does not remain stationary. On the fifth beat, he advances the right foot and makes on it a rapid half-turn left, placing himself thereby between the two ladies. On the sixth beat, he joins the right foot to the left in the first position and sinks the heels. A slight inward and upward movement of the left hand at the beginning of the bar, and downward and outward at the half-bar, gives a graceful emphasis to this short reverence.

Figure III: Section 2

The movements in this section, consisting of sideways reprises, hand in hand, followed by a slow reverence are performed as described in section 2 of the first figure of the *Gioioso*.

How to Dance the Bassa Danza of Spain and Italy

VENUS TU M'AS PRIS

How to Dance the Bassa Danza of Spain and Italy

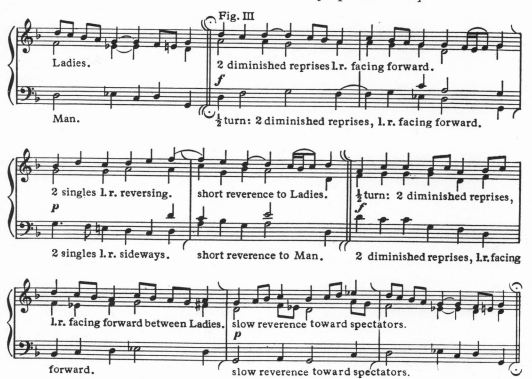

CHAPTER IV

Bassa et Alta

To Fabritio Caroso[1] we are indebted for the detailed record of an ancient Spanish *Bassa Danza* which, with its accompanying *Alta* and *Gioioso* movements, forms a complete suite. It is called by Caroso, *Balletto d'Incerto*, implying that it is of unknown date and origin.

The style of both music and dance are consistent with that of the middle of the fifteenth century. This curiously grave music, with its sombrely insistent rhythmic background, conjures up to the mind's eye a vision of the suave Spanish grace of Lucretia Borgia as, robed in shining garments of gold brocade, she danced hand in hand with her grim brother (César Borgia) before the Pope, Alexander VI, on the day of her marriage by proxy to Alfonso d'Este. She was said to possess such singular charm of expression and movement as made her appear yet more beautiful than she really was.[2]

The description of this dance given in Caroso's first book (*Il Ballarino*) is subsequently discounted in his second (*Nobilita dei Dame*)[3] as wholly incorrect; and a quite different version is substituted. The reader is repeatedly adjured not to perform it as formerly described, as this would be false. A detailed study of both texts makes it plain that the second version describes the original Spanish dance, while the first was merely an italianized invention quite out of character with the music.

In the Spanish dance the steps and movements, with the exception of the reprises, go to a measure of 3, 6, or 12 beats of a semibreve's length, in place of that of 2, 4, and 8, as prescribed in the italianized dance, and thus fit logically into the pattern of the music.

[1] *Il Ballarino*, 1581.   [2] *Lucretia Borgia*, F. Gregorovius, 1875.   [3] *Nobilita dei Dame*, 1600.

Bassa et Alta

THE BASSA DANZA

In the opening reverence (Caroso explains), although the dancers stand hand in hand, they should not face entirely forward, but turn obliquely towards each other (*un poco incontro*). Otherwise the man would appear to be ignoring his partner, as though he held her to be of no importance, which custom, he adds, has lingered among the Hebrews (*e questo uso e restato a gli Hebrei*). The reverence is followed by 2 continenzas in the same oblique position, after which the partners face forward for the passeggio, consisting of singles and doubles. During the intervening reprises and continenzas, however, they turn towards each other, so that they actually travel in opposite directions for the left-hand steps and come together again for the right. The Grand Reverence which should conclude the *Bassa* is held over until the close of the *Finale*, following upon the gioioso, and consists of a short section of *bassa danza*. This arrangement, Caroso explains, is in accordance with the ancestral usage.

The order of the steps in the Bassa Danza

Grand Reverence (*riverenza grave*)	6 beats
2 medium continenzas (*continenze semi-grave*)	6 beats
2 Spanish singles (*passi puntati semi-grave*) l.r.	6 beats
4 French doubles (*doppi finti à la Francese*) l.r.l.r.	24 beats
2 Spanish singles l.r.	6 beats
2 medium continenzas l.r.	6 beats
4 diminished reprises (*riprese minuite*) l.l.r.r.	8 beats
1 slow continenza (*continenza grave*) l.	6 beats
4 diminished reprises r.r.l.l.	8 beats
2 Spanish singles r.l.	6 beats
2 French doubles r.l.	12 beats
2 Spanish singles r.l.	6 beats
4 diminished reprises r.r.l.l.	8 beats
1 slow continenza r.	6 beats
4 diminished reprises l.l.r.r.	8 beats
2 medium continenzas l.r.	6 beats
Closing half-reverence	1 beat

HOW TO PERFORM THE STEPS

The Grand Reverence: The music starts with an anticipatory half-beat which may be used to advance the left foot a few inches. Caroso, who remarks that this kind of reverence is peculiar to the *Bassa et Alta* and the *Tordion*,[1] directs that the toe of the left foot while

---

[1] Termed *Tordiglione* by the Italians.

thus advanced should be raised a little from the ground. During the first and second beats (lowering the toe and raising the heel), draw back the left foot till the toe is level with the right heel and distant four inches in width, inclining the body. On the third beat, bend both knees outwards and on the fourth beat straighten them again. On the fifth beat, join up the left foot to the right in the third position (right), rising on the toes with body erect. On the sixth beat, sink the heels.

The arm movements: If the man is wearing a hat, he draws his left hand inward and upward during the first and second beats and removes his hat by the brim, holding it with the inside turned towards himself. During the third and fourth beats, with a graceful gesture, he draws it downward and outward. Then, during the remaining 2 beats, after returning it with an inward and upward movement, he replaces it firmly on his head.

The lady makes similar movements in a lesser degree, just drawing the left forearm inward and raising the hand, and then lowering the hand and arm outward, with a graceful turn of the wrist. The man will do likewise if he is not wearing a hat.

The medium continenzas: On the first beat, step sideways on the flat of the left foot a distance of four or five inches, bending the knees and swaying the left hip sideways. During the second beat, rise gently on the toes, turning the head towards the right. On the third beat, join the right foot to the left in the first position, making a dipping movement, with knees bent outward. At the half-bar, rise again on the toes and sink heels at the close. Perform the right continenza in similar fashion, beginning with the right foot and moving in the opposite direction. In common with the reverence just described, this type of continenza is said by Caroso to belong exclusively to the *Bassa et Alta* and the *Tordion*. Each continenza takes 3 semibreve beats.

The Spanish singles: We are told that this kind of single (named by Caroso *passo puntato semigrave*) is employed in *Bassa et Alta*, but in no other kinds of *balletti*, and that each single takes 3 semibreve beats. Standing with feet joined in the third position right and heels raised, turn the body (from the waist upwards) towards the right, so that the left shoulder points forward, and let the head face forward in line with the left shoulder. On the first beat step forward (but obliquely leftwards) on the flat of the left foot and rise smoothly on to the toes. On the second beat, join the right foot to the left in the first position and simultaneously make a dipping movement, bending both knees outwards. On the third beat, rise on the toes; and at the half-beat, make a quarter-turn leftward, so as to assume the third position left, with the head and right shoulder facing forward preparatory to making the right single. As you step on the first beat the hip on that side should be gently swayed outward. This swaying movement is described by Caroso as *pavoneggiandosi* in allusion to the proud deploying gesture of the peacock.

The arm movements: During the first 2 beats of the left single, move the free arm leftwards, from the elbow, raising the hand at the close. On the third beat, as you rise on the toes, move it back again towards the right with a graceful curving motion, once more raising the hand at the end. In making the right single, move the hand towards the right and back again leftwards.

The French doubles which follow after the Spanish singles are termed by Caroso *Doppi finti à la Francese* (feigned doubles), owing to the fact that the advancing steps are partially discounted by the two preliminary backward leaps, thus checking the progress.

The French feigned double: This ornamented double occupies 6 beats. On the first beat, make a left leap (sideways and backward) landing with the left toe on a level with the right heel and raising the right foot in front of the left. At the half-beat, make a sideways and backward leap with the right foot. On the second beat, step forward on the left toe with straightened knee, and on the third beat make a similar forward step on right toe. On the fourth beat (turning a little to the right, and with the head and left shoulder facing forward), step forward obliquely leftwards on the flat of the left foot, rising immediately on the toes and swaying the left hip outwards. On the fifth beat, join the right foot to the left in the first position and simultaneously make a dipping movement, bending both knees outwards. On the sixth beat, rise on the toes and turn, so as to face forward for the start of the right French double which is made in similar fashion, beginning with the right foot.

The arm movements: During the first 3 beats these should consist merely of a slight sideways movement to and fro of the free hand. During the remaining 3 beats, the arm movements will resemble those explained in connection with the Spanish single.

The diminished reprise: This kind of reprise, called *minuita* or *presta*, is a very ornate step, which was much in favour in southern countries. It appears to have been of African origin, since it has survived among American negro dancers. It consists of a sideways progression by means of the alternate closing and opening of the toes and heels in rapid succession. Let me first explain that the normal first position, with heels joined and toes separated, has its counterpart in the first *false* position, wherein the *toes* are joined and the heels separated. Standing therefore with feet joined in the normal first position and about to travel leftwards, move (in that direction) the left heel and the right toe. You will now be standing in the first *false* position, with toes joined and heels apart. Move next (in the same direction) the left toe and the right heel, which will bring you once more into the normal first position, but removed several inches farther to the left. This manoeuvre may conveniently be termed a *double twist.* Four of these go to one reprise, occupying 2 semibreve beats or bars. When the dancer has acquired great agility, it becomes unnecessary to count the beats, which will ripple along with easy fluency. To make the right reprise, move first the right heel and left toe towards the right. The movements of the feet should be small and the body held upright and motionless. The smoothly sailing effect is enhanced if the head and forearm are pointing in the opposite direction from that in which the dancer is travelling. The reprises go in pairs each way; namely, first two to the left and then two to the right or the reverse, as the case may be.

The slow continenza: This isolated slow continenza is performed in the same manner as the preceding medium continenzas, but with each movement occupying double the length of time, so that 1 continenza only is performed in the space of two.

ALTA DANZA

Whereas in the *Bassa Danza* each beat occupies a whole bar, the time measure of the *Alta Danza* is counted in bars of *2 minim beats* each. The opening Grand Reverence is, however, slow and formal, as though forming part of the *Bassa Danza*. In the rest of the dance, the steps are quick and light. The dancers stand at the foot of the dance, facing the spectators, and, having completed the reverence, advance hand in hand by means of 6 composite steps. This type of step, which resembles a French *fleuret*, is termed by Caroso a *seguito ordinario* (or ordinary sequence). During the last of these, the man guides the lady in a semicircular direction till she comes to rest opposite to him. After a mutual inclination she stands at ease while the man dances a stationary figure, called a *mutanza*, before her, making a series of steps turned alternately towards the left and right. He concludes with a half-reverence as a closing salutation. He stands at ease, while his partner repeats the same figure, and then himself has another short solo consisting of the same series of steps beginning with the right foot, turning first towards the right and then towards the left. The lady in her turn performs the same figure. This complete the *Alta*.

The order of the steps in the Alta Danza

Grand Reverence (*riverenza grave*)	6 bars
6 ordinary sequences (*seguiti ordinari*)	12 bars
Man: 2 ordinary sequences to left and right	4 bars
2 side-leaps (*trabucchetti*)	2 bars
1 feigned sequence (*seguito finto*) forward	2 bars
Half-reverence	1 bar
Lady: 2 ordinary sequences to left and right	4 bars
2 side-leaps	2 bars
1 feigned sequence forward	2 bars
Half-reverence.	
Man: repeats his solo, starting with right foot.	
Lady: repeats her solo, starting with right foot.	

HOW TO PERFORM THE STEPS OF THE ALTA

The Grand Reverence: Advance the left foot a few inches, with the heel resting on the ground and the toe a little raised. During the first 2 bars, draw back the left foot (resting the toe on the ground and raising the heel a little) until the toe comes level with back of the right heel. At the third bar, bend both knees outwards, inclining the head and body. At the fourth bar, straighten the knees; and at the fifth bar, join up the left foot to the right in the third position right, simultaneously rising on the toes and drawing the body erect. At the sixth bar, sink the heels. The arm movements are as described for the beginning of the *Bassa Danza*, but should be more moderate in scope; and there is no need for the man to remove his hat. During this reverence the partners stand side by side, yet turning obliquely towards each other.

The ordinary sequence: Each sequence occupies two bars of the *Alta Danza*. The dancers advance hand in hand, starting with the left foot. On the first beat, make a short springy step landing on the left toe, and on the second beat make a similar step landing on the right toe, so placed that the middle of the right foot is on a level with the left toe. The knees should be straightened during these 2 little steps. On the first beat of the second bar step forward again with the left foot, but this time treading on the flat of the foot, with the knee slightly bent. On the second beat, rise on the toes with straightened knees. Follow with the right sequence.

The side-leaps: Prior to making the left side-leap (according to Caroso's directions) the dancer raises the right hip slightly and lowers the left. This is an anticipatory movement during which the head should be turned towards the left and the arms a little to the right. With the left leap (*trabuchetto*) he lands on the ball of the left foot, simultaneously turning the head towards the right and the arms leftward (raising the left hip and lowering the right). As he lands, the right foot should be joined to the left, not touching the ground but held in the air and slightly advanced. The knees should be very straight and taut. The dancer is now in position to make the corresponding right side-leap in similar manner. Each leap occupies 1 bar.

Feigned sequence: The seguito finto occupies the space of 2 bars. After the pair of trabuchetti the dancer will be standing on the right foot, with the left raised forward a few inches from the ground. On the first beat draw it back, placing it in the fifth position right, with the toe on the ground and the heel raised, and inclining the body, as though making a semi-curtsy: at the *half-beat*, raise the right foot forward. On the second beat, draw back the right foot, placing the toe behind the left heel: at the *half-beat*, raise the left foot forward. On the first beat of the second bar, step forward on the flat of the left foot, bringing it level with its original position. On the second beat of the second bar, raise the right foot forward, in readiness for the performance of the right seguito finto.

The half-reverence: This occupies 1 bar. Draw back the left foot behind the right heel, bending both knees outwards. At the *half-bar*, join the right foot to the left in the first position, rising on the toes. Sink the heels at the close.

THE GIOIOSO FIGURE

Caroso directs that this figure shall be performed by the man before his partner and afterwards be repeated by the lady in similar fashion. To begin with, he advances sideways with a composite step designated by Caroso as a destice. This consists of 4 left underfoot steps followed by a left side-leap and a half-turn left, occupying the sixth bar. This series constitutes a double reprise left. The same movements are made with the right foot, and complete the advance. On the last bar a quarter-turn only should be made on the right foot, so as to face forward for the 2 continenzas which follow.

Next come 2 continenzas, 2 Spanish side-singles in retreat, and 2 Spanish doubles facing forward and advancing towards partner. Then 2 continenzas, 2 destice in retreat, 2 Spanish singles (advancing or retreating) and the Grand Reverence.

The lady is warned not to remain rigid like a statue while her partner dances before her, but to stand at ease, making various gracious movements. Nothing is said on this subject concerning her partner.

The order of the steps in the Gioioso

2 underfoot reprises l.; leap l. (destice)	
2 underfoot reprises l.; leap r. (destice)	12 bars
2 continenzas l.	6 bars
2 Spanish side-singles l.r.	6 bars
2 Spanish doubles l.r.	12 bars
2 continenzas l.r.	6 bars
2 underfoot reprises l.; leap l. (destice)	
2 underfoot reprises r.; leap r. (destice)	12 bars
2 Spanish singles l.r.	6 bars
(Grand Reverence)	6 bars

HOW TO PERFORM THE GIOIOSO STEPS

The odd half-bar at the opening of the gioioso figure may be used by the dancers to take up their respective positions, facing each other at a distance of about six feet.

The destice: The composite step, so named by Caroso, consists of 4 underfoot steps (*riprese sottopiede*) and 1 sideways-leap (*trabuchetto*). It occupies 6 bars each way, and is performed sideways. It makes a good effect if the head is turned in the direction in which the dancer is moving, while the arms are held in the opposite direction. To make the left destice, turn left shoulder to partner. On the first beat of the first bar, spring lightly sideways on to the left foot, raising the right foot backwards: at the *half-bar*, insert the right toe beneath the left heel, projecting the left foot forward. On the second bar, spring again sideways on to the left foot, raising the right foot backwards; and at the *half-bar*, insert the

40

right toe beneath the left heel, projecting the left foot forward. This completes the first left reprise. During the third and fourth bars, make the second left reprise in the same manner. The fifth and sixth bars are allotted to the trabuchetto. On the fifth bar, leap sideways smartly on to the left toe and raise the right foot forward with well-pointed toe and both knees straight and taut. Remain thus throughout the bar, making a half-turn left on the sixth bar, so as to have the right shoulder turned towards partner and the right foot still raised forward, ready for the right destice. In order to economize the space available for this advance, the left destice may diverge obliquely towards the left and the right one towards the right in zigzag fashion. At the close, a quarter-turn right, on the right toe, brings the dancer into position, facing partner for the pair of continenzas.

The two continenzas: This movement, as performed in the *Bassa et Alta*, occupies 3 bars to the left and 3 to the right. On the first beat of the first bar (looking over towards the left), move the left foot sideways, with pointed toe and straightened knee, and the weight resting firmly on the right foot. Remain thus throughout the bar. On the first beat of the second bar, transfer the weight to the left foot, rising on the toes and swaying the left hip outwards, turning the head to the right. Remain thus throughout the bar. On the first beat of the third bar, join the right foot to the left, in the first position, still remaining on the toes, and on the second beat, sink the heels. The arms should move in the opposite direction from that of the head, with a gently curving motion. This completes the left continenza. The right continenza should be made in similar fashion, starting with the right foot, and moving towards the right.[1]

Spanish side-singles in retreat: Each of these singles occupies 3 bars. At the close of the 2 continenzas, as you sink the heels, make a quarter-turn left, so as to have the right shoulder turned towards partner, and raise the left foot forward. On the first beat of the first bar, step sideways on the flat of the left foot, and on the second beat, rise on the toes. On the first beat of the second bar, join the right foot to the left in the first position, and on the second beat, make a dipping movement, bending both knees outwards. On the first beat of the third bar, rising on the left toe, and raising the right foot forward, make a half-turn to the right, so that the left shoulder is now turned towards partner. On the second beat, sink the left heel; but still keep the right foot raised a few inches from the ground in readiness for the right side-single (made in similar fashion), which completes the retreat. On the first beat of the final bar thereof, as you rise on the right toe, make a half-turn left, so as to turn right shoulder to partner for the first of the 2 Spanish doubles. These are made parading before partner to left and right.

Spanish doubles: Caroso informs us that the Spanish double is peculiar to the *Ballo* known as *Bassa et Alta di Castiglia*. This step is ornamented with flourishes and is therefore especially suitable to the gioioso figure of this dance. In his formula of steps, however, Caroso specifies *French* doubles. I conclude that this is an alternative name for the same step, since the only kind of French double mentioned in the preliminary treatise is a

[1] This manner of performing the continenza is peculiar to this dance.

doppio finto, as used in the opening movement of *Bassa et Alta*. I therefore choose the more ornate *Spanish* double for the lively gioioso. Each double occupies 6 bars. Standing on the right foot, with right shoulder turned towards partner and left foot raised forward, spring on to the left toe, simultaneously drawing it back level with the right and advancing the right, held in the air, a few inches off the ground. This occupies the first beat of bar one: on the second beat, spring on to the right toe, drawing it back level with the left and advancing the left held in the air some few inches off the ground. On the first beat of the second bar, step on to the flat of the left foot, and on the second beat, raise the right foot forward about knee high. This constitutes a left 'flourish'. During the third and fourth bars, make a right flourish in similar fashion, beginning with the right foot. On the first beat of bar five (still keeping right shoulder towards partner), step forward, a little towards your left, on the flat of the left foot, swaying sideways in that direction and moving the arms leftwards in a graceful curve. On the second beat, rise on the toes. On the first beat of bar six, join the right foot to the left in the fifth position, and on the second beat, make a rapid half-turn right, raising the right foot forward in readiness for the right Spanish double. On the second beat of the last bar thereof, make a quarter-turn left, so as to face partner for the closing Grand Reverence, and then sink the heels.

Grand Reverence: Standing with the left foot forward, draw it back during the first and second bars till the toe is level with the right heel and about four inches apart, inclining the head and body. At the third bar bend the knees outward, and at the fourth bar straighten them. At the fifth bar join the left foot to the right in the first position, rising on the toes. At the sixth bar, make a quarter-turn left and sink the heels.

Finale

The Finale, although performed to the music of the opening *Bassa Danza*, is actually a lively movement such as was commonly used to round off the *Balletto* or suite of dance movements. Standing face to face, but a few feet apart, the two dancers make a pair of destice (l.r.). They follow on with two ordinary singles and two ordinary sequences, approaching each other zigzag fashion. The man makes a half-reverence and kisses the lady's right hand. He then raises it shoulder high as (following a semicircular course) they change places by means of a gliding sequence called a *seguito scorso* (plural, *seguiti scorsi*), beginning with the left foot. He then takes her left hand in his own left, and, by means of a second seguito scorso, beginning with the right foot, they return to their original positions. Releasing hands, they then perform another pair of destice, facing each other, at the close of which the man makes a quarter-turn left and the lady a quarter-turn right so that the partners now face forward. They advance or retreat as preferred, hand in hand, with 2 ordinary singles. Then turning obliquely towards each other, they perform the final Grand Reverence.

Bassa et Alta

The order of the steps in the Finale

2 underfoot reprises l. and leap l. (destice)	6 bars
2 underfoot reprises r. and leap r. (destice)	6 bars
2 ordinary singles l.r.	4 bars
2 ordinary sequences l.r.	4 bars
1 half-reverence	2 bars
2 gliding sequences l.r.	4 bars
2 underfoot reprises l. and leap l.	6 bars
2 underfoot reprises r. and leap r.	6 bars
2 ordinary singles l.r.	4 bars
Grand Reverence	6 bars

HOW TO PERFORM THE STEPS

The destice: These will be performed as described for the gioioso figure.

The ordinary singles: This type of single, which, in his second book,[1] Caroso terms *puntato breve*, occupy only 2 bars each. To make a left single, advance the left foot lightly on the first beat of the first bar, with well-pointed toe, but still keeping the weight resting on the right foot. On the second beat of the bar, transfer the weight on to the flat of the left foot. On the first beat of the second bar, join up the right foot to the left in the third position left, simultaneously making a dipping movement, with the knees bent outwards. On the second beat, rise on the toes with straightened knees, and on the half-beat, sink the left heel, throwing all the weight on to the left foot, and thus releasing the right, which should be raised a little off the ground in preparation for the right single. This manner of performing the singles is peculiar to this dance.

Arm movements: During the first bar, look over towards the left foot and hold the arms (slightly bent) in the opposite direction. During the second bar, turn the face forward and, with a graceful, curving motion, bring the arms over to the left side. These movements should melt imperceptibly into one another in a natural manner.

The ordinary sequence: This sequence, called *seguito ordinario*, occupies 2 bars and usually occurs in pairs (l.r.). Technically, it amounts to the same thing as a flourish. To make the left sequence, spring forward lightly on to the left toe (which has previously been raised a little off the ground). On the second beat of the first bar, make a similar springy half-step on to the right toe. Each of these steps should be so measured that the heel comes level with the middle of the stationary foot. On the first beat of the second bar, step forward on to the flat of the left foot, and on the second beat raise the right foot a little forward in readiness for the right sequence.

The half-reverence and the *closing Grand Reverence* should be performed as already

[1] *Nobilita dei Dame.*

43

explained in the preceding figures. Should the man be in costume and wearing a hat, he would remove and deftly replace the hat during these ceremonious salutations.

I would here explain that in this elaborate *balletto* and also in the *Tordiglione*, as both are described in *Nobilita dei Dame*, Caroso uses a peculiar system of nomenclature for his composite steps and also changes the gender of certain figures and names of simple steps. For all other dances as described by him, I propose to revert to the more convenient basic names as used in his first treatise, *Il Ballarino*.

BASSA ET ALTA

Grand Reverence ....: 2 medium

continenzas (right) (left)...: 2 Spanish singles (left) ....

(right)...................................: 4 French doubles (left)...

Bassa et Alta

.... (right) .... (left) ....

.... (right) ....

.... 2 Spanish singles (left) .... (right) ....

2 medium continenzas (left) ..... (right) .... 4 diminished reprises

(left, left) .... (right, right) .... 1 slow continenza,

Bassa et Alta

46

Bassa et Alta

1 slow continenza(right)

4 diminished reprises (l.l.)   (r.r.)

2 medium continenzas(l.)   (r.)   ½ revce
front.

○=72

Grand Reverence   left sequence

r. sequence   l. sequence   r. sequence   l. sequence

47

Bassa et Alta

r. sequence........: 2 sequences: to left and right.   2 side leaps (l. r.)

1 feigned sequence (l.)   ½ Reverence, 2 sequences: to left, and right ....:

2 side leaps (l. r.)   1 feigned sequence (l.)   ½ Rev.ᶜᵉ 2 sequences (to right and left) ....

........: 2 side leaps (r. l.)   1 feigned sequence (r.)   ½ Rev.ᶜᵉ 2 sequences (to right and

left) ....: 2 side leaps (r. l.)   1 feigned sequence (r.) ½ Rev.ᶜᵉ left (underfoot)

48

Bassa et Alta

reprise..............................: left leap.............. right(underfoot) reprise..............

..............: right leap.............: 2 continenzas (left)............(right)..............

..............: 2 side Spanish-singles. (l.)................. (r.)..............:

2 Spanish doubles crossways. (l.) ....:(r.) ....

....: 2 continenzas (l.).................:(r.) ....

49

Bassa et Alta

............: left (underfoot) reprise.........................: left leap................: right (under-

-foot) reprise.........................: right leap. 2 forward Spanish-singles (l.)......(r.)............

............: Grand Reverence...:

left (underfoot) reprise.........................: left leap. ....: right(under-

-foot) reprise.........................: right leap............: 2 ordinary singles (l.r.)................

50

Bassa et Alta

left sequence......: right sequence......: ½ reverence........: 2 gliding sequences...............

..............: left (underfoot) reprise ....: left leap...............: right

(underfoot) reprise...............: right leap......................: 2 ordinary singles (l.r.)..

..............................: Grand Reverence...:

CHAPTER V

The Canaries

THOINOT ARBEAU (Jehan Tabourot), in his treatise named *Orchésographie* (1589), likens the *Canaries* to the Spanish *Pavan*, as being a dance of very similar type. He is right in the sense that the *Canaries*, though claimed to have been derived from a dance in use among the native Canary Islanders, had inevitably, in course of time, become adapted to the Spanish temperament; and so, in like manner, had the Spanish *Pavan* (originally derived from the stately *Pavana Italiana*) become transformed into a spirited Spanish dance containing alternate challenging advances and sudden retreats. With regard to the *Canaries*, Arbeau concedes that these advancing and retreating passages are 'gaillards, et neantmoins estranges, bizares, et qui resentent fort le sauvage' (original spelling). When he comes, however, to detailed information concerning the performance of this dance, Arbeau restricts himself to a single passage, telling his pupil Capriol that he will be able to learn others from those who know them, or even to invent some for himself! Happily this lack of detail on his part is amply compensated for in the treatises of Caroso and Negri, who both purport to give us the Dances of France, Spain and Italy.[1] All the early Canary tunes are highly characteristic, and exercise a strange fascination on both listener and dancer. We will begin with the version of this dance given by Cesare Negri, arranged for two dancers.

IL CANARIO (CESARE NEGRI)

The dance opens with the medium reverence and 2 continenzas, wherein the partners stand side by side facing the onlookers, yet obliquely turned towards each other. This formal salutation occupies the first strain of 8 bars. The second strain of 8 bars consists of 4 sliding broken-sequences (termed *seguiti spezzati schisciati*), advancing hand in hand

[1] *Il Ballarino*, Fabritio Caroso, 1581; *Nuove Inventione di Balli*, Cesare Negri, 1604.

52

towards the centre of the dance. The partners now release hands and, linking their right arms, they revolve towards the right with 4 more broken-sequences, which occupy the third strain. During the fourth strain, they link their left arms and revolve to the left in the same manner. During the fifth strain, releasing their hold with a rapid half-reverence, they go to opposite ends of the dance, the lady towards the front, veering towards the left and facing back stage, and the man to the back, veering towards the right and facing forward, thus ending up face to face (at an oblique angle as regards the spectators), and about eight feet apart. In taking up their positions, they each turn to their left and follow the pattern of the letter S, the man as though beginning at the top and working downwards, and the lady as though at the tail and working upwards. In making this evolution they progress by means of 4 sliding broken-sequences, as throughout the preceding strains. In the sixth strain, making a rapid quarter-turn right on the right toe, they then describe a circle to the left in sliding broken-sequences. In completing the final sequence, they should make 2 rapid half-steps forward and a little jump (called the cadenza), so as to land on the last beat of the bar with feet joined in the first position. After the termination of the sixth strain, there is a final chord during which the dancers make a medium reverence towards each other.

MAN'S FIRST VARIATION (*Mutanza*)

The lady stands at ease while her partner dances before her. He opens with a circle to the left consisting of 4 sliding broken-sequences, the last of which terminates with 2 half-steps forward and the cadenza. This completes the first strain. In the second strain, all the steps are made by the left foot, and the reprise moves leftward. Turning his left shoulder to partner, he makes a high backward slide with the foot, tapping the ground in passing (likened by Arbeau to the action of killing a spider), followed by a stamp behind the right heel: these actions are repeated. The second half of the strain is occupied by 2 beaten sequences (*seguiti battuti*) and one left diminished reprise (approaching partner sideways), closing the strain with a rapid half-turn left, on the ball of the left foot. The dancer now stands with his right shoulder towards partner, ready for the third strain. This consists of the same series of steps as those occupying the second strain, but using the right foot in place of the left. This completes the advance. During the fourth strain, with right shoulder still turned towards partner, the dancer makes a double diminished reprise leftwards, retreating sideways, and a rapid half-turn *right*, on the left foot. This occupies half the strain. During the second half, with left shoulder turned to partner, he makes another double reprise, toward his right. In the fifth strain, facing partner, he completes his retreat with five backward stamps starting with the left foot and five more starting with the right. The sixth strain is occupied by the left circle in sliding broken-sequences, as at the beginning; and during the final chord both dancers salute each other with a short reverence.

The Canaries

LADY'S FIRST VARIATION

The lady starts by circling to the left with 4 sliding broken-sequences, concluding with 2 half-steps and the left cadenza. Her second strain consists of 8 beaten sequences (*seguiti battuti*) advancing towards partner. These occupy 1 bar each and are peculiar to the canaries. In the third strain, still facing partner, she makes 2 double diminished reprises crossways (l.r.). In the fourth strain she describes 2 circles first to the left and then to the right by means of gliding-sequences of little half-steps (*scorsi*), coming to rest directly in front of her partner. During the fifth strain she effects her retreat with 4 slow backward steps (*passi grave*), giving a stamp with each and then pointing the toe of the forward foot on the second beat. In the sixth strain she makes 2 side-leaps (l.r.) facing partner and then, turning obliquely leftward, 1 diminished reprise (l.). Facing partner, she makes 2 more side-leaps (r.l.) and, turning obliquely to the right, 1 diminished reprise (r.) with reverence towards partner, in which he joins, on final chord.

INTERMEDIATE PASSEGGIO

Throughout the passeggio the partners dance simultaneously, progressing by means of the sliding broken-sequences. They finish by changing places, the man passing to the front of the stage and the lady to the back. I use the term 'stage' to represent the dancing space, although there may not actually be a raised platform, as this is a convenient way of describing various evolutions and changes of position.

In the first strain, the dancers circle to their left with 4 sliding broken-sequences starting with the left foot. In the second strain, they advance towards each other in zigzag fashion, swerving alternately to left and right, so as to meet in the centre of the dance at the close of the strain. In the third strain, linking their right arms, they revolve to the right with 4 broken-sequences; and in the fourth strain they link the left arms and revolve to the left. During the fifth strain, describing the figure S, as at the beginning the man travels to the front of the stage and the lady to the back. They should take up their position slightly aslant as before, so that the man is not entirely placed with his back to the spectators, nor screening his partner from their view. The sixth strain is occupied by the left circle, 2 half-steps and cadenza, with reverence on the final chord.

MAN'S SECOND VARIATION

Facing partner, the man makes 6 heel-and-toe steps with the left foot and left cadenza. This is followed by 2 slow steps advancing (l.r.) and 2 beaten sequences (l.r.). This completes the first strain. The same series of steps is repeated during the second strain, starting with the right foot. At the close he makes a rapid quarter-turn left on the left toe, so as to have his right shoulder turned to partner during the third strain. He approaches her with a right diminished reprise; then, swinging round with a half-turn right on his right toe and turning left shoulder to partner, he continues to advance with a left diminished

IL CANARIO

reprise. This occupies the first half of the third strain. During the second half, making a rapid quarter-turn left on the right toe, so as to face partner, he performs 2 backward flourishes (*reccaciate*) and 2 beaten-sequences which bring us to the end of the third strain. During the fourth strain, making a rapid quarter-turn left, on the right toe, and turning right shoulder to partner, he makes 3 presto taps with the left foot (heel, toe, heel), the weight resting on the right foot. This occupies 1 bar, and is followed by 2 sideways-leaps (*trabuchetti*) l.r. and 1 hop, landing with the feet joined in the first position. This occupies the first half of the strain. He then makes a swift half-turn right, on the left foot, trailing the right foot lightly round till it comes to rest beside the left, in the first position. In the second half of the strain, the same series of steps is repeated (the left shoulder being now turned to partner), using the right foot in place of the left. The fifth strain is a repetition of the same formula as that used in the fourth, turning first the right shoulder to partner and then the left. This concludes the retreat. The sixth strain is occupied by the leftward circle terminating in the 2 half-steps and left cadenza, followed by the mutual reverence on the final chord.

LADY'S SECOND VARIATION

The lady opens with the leftward circle terminating in the 2 half-steps and cadenza. At the close she turns her left shoulder to partner in preparation for a sideways advance. The second strain starts with 3 sideways-leaps (l.r.l.), called trabuchetti, ending with the joining of the feet, on the fourth beat, in the fifth position right. Immediately, however, she makes a swift quarter-turn left on both feet, facing partner with joined feet for the second half of the strain. This consists of 2 diminished reprises (r.l.), which bring us to the end of the second strain. She makes a quarter-turn left on the left toe, so that her right shoulder is turned to partner. During the third strain she repeats the same series of steps as those occupying the second strain, but starting with the right foot, and making a quarter-turn right on the right toe, to face partner for the second half of the strain. The two reprises are made to left and right. In the fourth strain she describes 2 circles in front of her partner (l.r.) by means of the little half-steps on the toes termed gliding-sequences (*scorsi*), facing him at the close. This completes the advance. In the fifth strain, the retreat (*ritirata*) begins. Standing with the left foot behind the right heel, in the third position right, the lady gives 4 stamps (l.r.l.r.), followed by a rapid quarter-turn left on the right toe, thus turning her right shoulder to partner. She then makes a sideways retreat by means of a double diminished reprise (left), which brings us to the end of the fifth strain. At the close she makes a swift quarter-turn right on the left toe so as to face partner and carries the right foot lightly round behind the left heel, in the third position left. In the sixth strain she gives 4 stamps (r.l.r.l.), and then, making a quarter-turn right on the left toe, thus turning left shoulder to partner, she completes her retreat with a double diminished reprise (right). Then, turning to face partner, she makes the reverence in company with him on the final chord.

FINALE

In this closing passeggio both dancers take part, employing the sliding broken-sequences throughout. During the opening strain, they circle to their left, completing the fourth sequence with 2 half-steps and a left cadenza. In the second strain, they approach each other in zigzag fashion (l.r.l.r.), meeting in the centre of the dance at the completion of the strain. During the third strain, linking their right arms, they revolve to the right. In the fourth strain, they link their left arms and revolve to the left. They separate, and make their way independently (following a semicircular path) towards back stage. Here they resume their original positions, standing side by side and facing forward, with the lady on the man's right. Turning towards each other, they perform the Grand Reverence which occupies the whole of the sixth strain. On the final chord, they turn to face the onlookers and perform a short reverence with grace and decorum.

The order of the steps

Opening passeggio

First strain:
Medium reverence	4 bars
2 continenzas l.r.	4 bars

Second strain:
4 sliding broken-sequences, advancing	8 bars

Third strain:
4 sliding broken-sequences, revolving right	8 bars

Fourth strain:
4 sliding broken-sequences, revolving left	8 bars

Fifth strain:
4 sliding broken-sequences, in figure S	8 bars

Sixth strain:
4 sliding broken-sequences, circling left	8 bars

Short reverence on final chord.

The Canaries

Man's first variation (*mutanza*)

First strain:

4 sliding broken-sequences, circling left	8 bars

Second strain (sideways advance l.):

Backslide, stamp; backslide, stamp (l.)	4 bars
2 beaten-sequences l.	2 bars
1 diminished reprise l.	2 bars

Third strain (sideways advance r.):

Backslide, stamp; backslide, stamp (r.)	4 bars
2 beaten-sequences r.	2 bars
1 diminished reprise r.	2 bars

Fourth strain (sideways retreat):

1 double reprise l., 1 double reprise r.	8 bars

Fifth strain (backward retreat):

2 backward stamps l.r.	2 bars
2 stationary stamps l.r.l.	2 bars
2 backward stamps r.l.	2 bars
3 stationary stamps r.l.r.	2 bars

Sixth strain:

4 sliding broken-sequences, circling left	8 bars

Short reverence on final chord.

Lady's first variation

First strain:

4 sliding broken-sequences, circling left	8 bars

Second strain (frontal advance):

8 beaten-sequences l.r.	8 bars

Third strain:

Double diminished reprise, traversing (l.)	4 bars
Double diminished reprise, traversing (r.)	4 bars

Fourth strain:

Gliding-sequence (*scorsa*), circling left	4 bars
Gliding-sequence (*scorsa*), circling right	4 bars

Fifth strain (zigzag retreat):

4 slow steps (*passi gravi*), backward	8 bars

Sixth strain:

2 side-leaps l.r. and 1 diminished reprise l.	4 bars
2 side-leaps r.l. and 1 diminished reprise r.	4 bars

Short reverence on final chord.

The Canaries

Intermediate passeggio

First strain:
    4 sliding broken-sequences, circling left   8 bars
Second strain:
    4 sliding broken-sequences, advancing zigzag   8 bars
Third strain:
    4 sliding broken-sequences, revolving right   8 bars
Fourth strain:
    4 sliding broken-sequences, revolving left   8 bars
Fifth strain:
    4 sliding broken-sequences, changing places   8 bars
Sixth strain:
    4 sliding broken-sequences, circling left   8 bars
Short reverence on final chord.

Man's second variation

First strain (advance):
    6 heel and toe steps and cadenza l.   4 bars
    2 forward steps; 2 beaten-sequences l.r.   4 bars
Second strain:
    6 heel-and-toe steps and cadenza r.   4 bars
    2 forward steps; 2 beaten-sequences r.l.   4 bars
Third strain (right shoulder to partner):
    1 diminished reprise right; half-turn r.   2 bars
    1 diminished reprise left; quarter-turn l.   2 bars
    2 backward flourishes l.r.   2 bars
    2 beaten-sequences l.r.   2 bars
Fourth strain (retreat: right shoulder to partner):
    3 taps (heel, toe, heel; left)   1 bar
    2 side-leaps l.r.; hop (joined feet)   3 bars
    (Right half-turn) 3 taps (heel, toe, heel; r.)   1 bar
    2 side-leaps r.l.; hop (joined feet)   3 bars
Fifth strain:
    Repeat the formula as in the preceding strain   8 bars
Sixth strain:
    4 sliding broken-sequences, circling left   8 bars
Short reverence on final chord.

The Canaries

Lady's second variation

First strain:	
4 sliding broken-sequences, circling left	8 bars
Second strain (advance: left shoulder to partner):	
3 side-leaps l.r.l., joined feet; quarter-turn left	4 bars
2 diminished reprises r.l.	4 bars
Third strain:	
3 side-leaps r.l.r.; joined feet; quarter-turn right	4 bars
2 diminished reprises l.r.	4 bars
Fourth strain:	
2 circles in gliding sequences	8 bars
Fifth strain (retreat: facing partner):	
4 stamps l.r.l.r.; quarter-turn left	4 bars
Double diminished reprise l.; quarter-turn right	4 bars
Sixth strain:	
4 stamps r.l.r.l.; quarter-turn right	4 bars
Double diminished reprise r.; quarter-turn left	4 bars

Short reverence on final chord.

FINALE

Passeggio for both dancers

First strain:	
4 sliding broken-sequences, circling left	8 bars
Second strain:	
4 sliding broken-sequences, advancing	8 bars
Third strain:	
4 sliding broken-sequences, revolving right	8 bars
Fourth strain:	
4 sliding broken-sequences, revolving left	8 bars
Fifth strain:	
4 sliding broken-sequences, describing a semicircle to back stage (man l., lady r.)	8 bars
Sixth strain:	
Grand Reverence towards each other	8 bars

Short reverence to onlookers on final chord.

The Canaries

Medium reverence: Standing on the right foot, with the left foot advanced a few inches, remain thus during the first bar. On the first beat of the second bar, draw back the left foot, so that the toe is level with the right heel, and incline the head and body. During the third bar, first bend the knees outwards and then, throwing the weight on to the left foot, straighten the right knee. On the first beat of the fourth bar restore the weight on to the right foot and, rising on the toes, join the left foot to it, raising the head and body. Sink the heels at the close. The Grand Reverence at the end of the dance is performed in a similar manner, but allowing twice the time for each movement, so that the whole reverence occupies 8 bars instead of 4.

The pair of continenzas: These occupy 4 bars together. On the first beat of the first bar, extend the left foot sideways a few inches, bending the knees outwards. On the first beat of the second bar, join the right foot to the left, rising on the toes, with straightened knees. Sink the heels at the close of the bar. During the third and fourth bars, perform the right continenza in similar fashion, beginning with the right foot and moving towards the right. The hip on the side towards which you are moving should be swayed outwards a little.

Sliding broken-sequence (seguito-spezzato schisciato): This is a lilting step, resembling the saltarello step, formerly called *pas de Brabant*, except that the feet slide along the ground instead of stepping. Each sequence occupies 2 bars of triple time. On the first beat of the first bar, slide the left foot forward, and on the third beat, rising on the toes, bring the right toe level with the left heel. On the first beat of the second bar, slide the left foot forward again, bending the knees and advancing the left hip a little. On the third beat, rise on the toes, but quickly sink the heels before beginning the right sequence. The dancer sways slightly towards the side of the advancing foot. Negri directs that these sliding sequences may be done *in saltino*, by which he means that a hop may be made on the third beat of the second bar. Caroso on the contrary makes them smoothly undulating, as we shall see in the next example, which is of an earlier date. The arms should be swung gently on the side of the advancing foot.

Backslide and stamp: These movements occupy 1 bar each. With the left foot raised forward, bring it down sharply on the first beat of bar one, sliding it backward so that it kicks out at the back. At the second bar, bring it down behind the right heel (third position right) with a smart stamp. This is done twice running in the man's first variation, taking 4 bars in all. Perform the corresponding right-hand movements in their turn with the right foot in place of the left. Negri gives no composite name to these movements, but specifies each in its turn, calling them *battute* (beats).

Beaten-sequence (seguito battuto): This sequence occupies 1 bar for each. On the first beat, standing on the right foot, slide the left heel forward (lifting the toe) till the foot is raised several inches from the ground. On the second beat, lower the toe and slide it backward till the foot is raised behind several inches from the ground. On the third beat, join it to the right foot in the first position with a smart stamp, thus accenting the third beat with a curious cross rhythm. Make the right beaten-sequence in similar fashion. Sometimes several such sequences are made in succession with the same foot.

Diminished reprise (ripresa minuita): This is a sideways movement. Stand with the feet joined in the first position. In order to move leftwards, extend in that direction the left heel and the right toe (so that the feet are now toe to toe, and with heels separated). Next, move leftward the left toe and the right heel, thus resuming the normal first position. These two movements constitute a 'double twist'. Make as many of these as the time allows for. The smaller the movements of the feet, the more of them can be made, in the manner of a rapid trill. When making a right reprise, move first the right heel and the left toe.

Backward stamps: These are made on the flat of the foot a few inches behind the heel of the forward foot, and turning the body a little from side to side, drawing the arms back, leftward for the left stamp, and to the right for the right stamp. In the case of the 3 quick stamps of 1 beat each, keep the arms towards the side of the foot which makes the first and last stamp. The head should be turned towards partner.

The gliding-sequence (scorso): This consists of little half-steps, made on the toes, with knees well straightened. According to whether the dancer is circling to left or right, the foot on that side should take the lead, the other foot only moving up to the heel of the forward foot. The head and arms should be turned in the reverse direction from that towards which the dancer moves, and the arms curved.

The slow backward steps: These occur in the retreat of the lady's first variation. They should be made in grandiose style, the retreating foot being placed with firm precision on the first beat of the first bar, stepping on the flat of the foot. The forward (stationary) foot, though touching the ground, should have no weight on it. On the first beat of the second bar, lift and lightly replace the forward foot, with toe well pointed. On the first beat of the succeeding bar, step backwards on it in the same manner as with the first foot. The arms should be drawn back on the side of the stepping foot, and gracefully curved. The head should be raised and turned in the direction of the forward foot. The body should be turned towards the side of the backward-stepping foot, turning from side to side in zig-zag fashion. This retreat is very effective, and emphasizes the fiery character of this dance.

Heel-and-toe steps: These occur in the man's second variation and occupy 4 bars. They are done by the one foot while the dancer hops on the other foot, each step being accompanied by a hop. On the first beat of the first bar, he puts his left heel to the ground beside the toe of the right foot. On the third beat of the same bar, he puts his toe down, level with the middle of the right foot. On the first beat of the second bar, he again poses the heel of the left foot beside the toe of the right, and on the third beat he crosses the left foot over the right, putting the toe to the ground on the other side of it. On the first beat of the third bar, he places the left heel beside the toe of the right foot, and on the third beat, he draws back the left foot, putting the toe to the ground beside the right heel. This makes the sixth step, or placing of the left foot. In anticipation of the fourth bar, he scoops it forward and jumps, drawing it back again so as to land with the feet joined in the first position, exactly on the first beat of the fourth bar, where he comes to rest. This kind of jump constitutes a left cadenza. During the second half of the strain, he performs the right heel-and-toe passage with right cadenza, in similar fashion.

The backward flourish (recacciate): This resembles the ordinary hopped flourish, with the difference that simultaneously with the first hop, the free (forward) foot is kicked backwards. Each flourish occupies 1 bar. For a left backward flourish, stand on the right foot with the left foot raised forward. On the first beat, hopping on the right toe, kick the left foot backwards. On the second beat, while remaining stationary on the right toe, put the left toe to the ground behind the right heel. On the third beat, slip the left toe springily under the right heel, chasing the right foot forward in the air, a few inches from the ground. To make the right flourish, as you hop on the left foot, kick the right foot backwards. This backward kick is called by Thoineau Arbeau a *ruade*, or 'horse's kick'. On the second beat, put the right toe to the ground behind the left heel; and on the third beat, slip it under the left heel, chasing the left foot forward. This kind of flourish is consequently named the *recacciata* or 'chasing step'.

The three taps: These are done presto in the space of one bar. Let the weight rest upon the right foot while the left foot drums with heel, toe and heel.

The two side-leaps (trabuchetti): These follow after the bar containing the 3 taps, and occupy 1 bar each (l.r.). When leaping to the left, land on the toe, raising the right foot forward in front of the left, with toe well pointed and knees straightened. Make the same kind of leap to the right, and after the concluding hop (occupying 1 bar), make a rapid half-turn right on the left foot, trailing the right foot round in front of the left, with no weight on it, and bringing it to rest beside the left in readiness for the repeat of this series of steps, beginning with the right foot.

The leftward circle and cadenza: Whenever the leftward circle is concluded by a cadenza, this must be taken out of the final right-sequence as follows (the broken-sequence occupying 2 bars). On the first beat of bar one, slide the right foot forward on the flat of the foot. On the third beat, rising on the toes, bring up the left toe behind the right heel. On the first beat of bar two, slide the right foot forward again on the flat of the foot. On the second beat, make 2 tiny half-steps (l.r.) on the toes: then, scooping the left foot forward, make a little jump. In descending, draw back the left foot so as to land on the third beat with feet joined in the first position.

The Grand Reverence: This is performed in the same manner as the medium reverence; but each movement takes double the time.

The Canaries

IL CANARIO (CESARE NEGRI)

The foregoing tune appears to have gained a wide popularity; for we meet with it in Arbeau's treatise[1] (wherein the triple time-measure has been converted into duple time) and again in the Straloch Lute Book[2] (in the usual triple time). It is to this latter version that we owe the three curious introductory strains which usher in the exuberant melody. Negri's arrangement of the dance allots distinct types of variations individually to the man and to the lady, from which I have chosen those that I find to be the most attractive and easily memorized. In the next example, as arranged by Caroso, there is no such distinction as to style, and the partners, treated on an equal footing, perform identical variations each in turn. From its earlier date one may infer that it approaches more nearly to the pristine Spanish *Canaries*. The tune is short and repeats itself *ad infinitum*; nevertheless, it does not tire the listener, who becomes somehow fascinated by its monotonous reiteration.

IL CANARIO (FABRITIO CAROSO)

This dance, in common with the preceding one, is described as for two dancers, although, no doubt, in large mixed gatherings there could be many couples performing it simultaneously. For general convenience, I will describe it as though performed by a single couple on a stage.

The dancers stand side by side, facing forward, but turned obliquely towards each other, with the lady on the man's right.

The measure of the tune consists of 16 bars of triple time and their repeat, thus making 32 bars in all. At the end of the repeat there is a chord for the cadenza. This terminates the double strain, there being no closing reverence as in Negri's version.

The dance opens with a reverence of 4 bars' duration, and a pair of continenzas occupying another 4 bars. The dancers then advance, hand in hand, with 4 sliding broken-sequences which complete the 16-bar strain. During the repeat, the man takes the lady's right hand in his own (holding it shoulder high) and they revolve to the right with 4 more sliding broken-sequences. Letting go hands, they continue turning in the same direction, with 2 more broken-sequences, so that the man is now facing back stage and the lady looking towards the front. With 2 further broken-sequences the man then makes his way to the back of the stage, curving round leftwards so as to take up his station in what is, for him, the right-hand corner, facing forward. The lady, pursuing a similar course front-

[1] *Orchésographie*, 1587.   [2] Manuscript in the Advocate's Library, Edinburgh, *c.* 1600.

wards, lands in the diagonally opposite corner (front stage) facing partner. They will thus have described a double hook, turning first right and then left. In order to avoid redundant explanations we will henceforth use the term 'double hook' to indicate this separating movement, when the partners release hands and take up their station facing each other a short distance apart. Similarly, the broken-sequences used throughout this dance will be understood to be sliding ones, this being the rule in the *Canaries*. The little hop at the end of each sequence, favoured by Negri, is absent in Caroso's version, there being merely the jump (called cadenza) on the final chord.

FIRST VARIATION (MUTANZA)

During the first 8 bars, the man approaches his partner with 8 beaten-sequences (*seguiti battuti*), after which, still facing her, he makes a double diminished reprise, to the left, and another to the right. This brings us to the end of the strain. During the first 8 bars of the repeat, he retreats with 4 slow steps (*passi gravi*) occupying 2 bars each; and during the remaining 8 bars, he describes a circle leftwards with 4 broken-sequences, ending with 2 little half-steps forward and a cadenza on the final chord.

This variation is repeated by the lady.

SECOND VARIATION

During the first 8 bars the man makes 8 beaten-sequences, two per foot alternately. When making the left pair (facing right), he turns his left shoulder to partner: and then, with a rapid half-turn left on the left foot, presents his right shoulder to her for the right-hand pair; and so on, turning right and left, for the other two pairs, which complete the sideways advance, gaining ground with each half-turn. During the second half of the strain, he begins his retreat. Keeping his right shoulder turned obliquely towards partner he performs 3 minim reprises (*riprese minime*) and one left side-leap (*trabuchetto*), retreating leftwards, followed by 3 right minim reprises and 1 right side-leap, turning obliquely towards the right. This brings us to the end of the strain and constitutes the first half of the retreat (*ritirata*). During the first 8 bars of the repeat the dancer completes his retreat, repeating the same actions as those already performed during the preceding 8 bars. The second half of the repeat is occupied by the 4 broken-sequences, circling left, followed by the cadenza on the final chord.

INTERMEDIATE PASSEGGIO

The partners approach each other swerving to left and right with 4 broken-sequences, arranging to meet in the centre, and adjusting their respective positions, if necessary, so as to come directly face to face. The man takes the lady's right hand in his own, raising it shoulder high, and they revolve to the right with 4 broken-sequences. This brings us to the end of the strain. At the repeat they release hands and continue circling in the same direction with 2 broken-sequences, after which the lady travels towards back stage with

2 more broken-sequences, curving leftwards to complete the 'double hook' and arriving at the position previously occupied by the man during the first part; whilst he, travelling in the same manner towards the front stage, arrives at the diagonally opposite corner (previously occupied by the lady). During the remaining 8 bars, they circle to the left with 4 broken-sequences followed by the cadenza on the final chord.

THIRD VARIATION

The man turns left shoulder to partner and performs 2 left beaten-sequences followed by 3 stamps (r.l.r.), in third position left, and 1 more left beaten-sequence. This series of steps occupies 4 bars. Making a rapid half-turn left on the left toe, so as to present right shoulder to partner, he repeats the same series of steps, but using the right foot in place of the left. During the second half of the strain, turning alternately to right and left, he repeats the entire procedure. This completes his advance, and brings us to the end of the strain. During the first 8 bars of the repeat, he makes his retreat as follows: Two backward, sliding steps occupying 1 bar each (l.r.) turning obliquely to left and right; followed by 1 backward broken-sequence (l.) turning obliquely left, and occupying 2 bars. The same series of steps is repeated, beginning with the right foot and turning obliquely right, left, right. This completes the first half of the repeat. The remaining 8 bars are devoted to the circle leftwards in broken-sequences, followed by the cadenza on the final chord. Carry the arms turned in the direction in which you are moving. The lady performs the same variation in turn.

FOURTH VARIATION

The man makes a quarter-turn to the right on the right toe, so as to have his left shoulder turned towards partner. The first 4 bars are devoted to a heel-and-toe passage performed entirely by the left foot. During the first bar, standing still on his right foot, he makes, with the left, 3 rapid scooping slides (heel, toe, heel) forward, backward and forward. In the second bar, he makes 1 slow backward slide (toe), raising the foot behind (this occupies the first and second beats), and 1 quick forward slide (heel), raising the foot forward (on the third beat). In the third bar he makes 3 rapid slides (toe, heel, toe), the first backward, crossing the left foot over the stationary right, the second one sliding forward, still crossed over the right, and the third backward in a straight line, in the normal position beside the right foot. On the first beat of the fourth bar, he makes a stamp on the flat of the left foot beside the right and holds this position during the rest of the bar. This completes the first 4 bars of the strain. During the next 4 bars, keeping the left shoulder to partner, he makes 3 beaten-sequences (r.l.r.) and 2 quick stamps (l.r.), springing sideways towards his partner, the first stamp being made with the left foot (as he lands from his spring) and the second following it *presto*, as he joins up the right foot. As he springs he should raise the left elbow outwards and turn his head leftwards. During the second half of the strain he makes a half-turn left on his left foot and repeats the whole series of actions which occupied the first half, turning his right shoulder to partner and using the right foot in place of the left. The first 8 bars of the repeat are devoted to the retreat, which is accomplished in the following manner: Keeping the right shoulder turned towards partner, the dancer makes one slow left reprise (*ripresa grave*) followed by 3 side-leaps (l.r.l.). This series of steps occupies 4 bars. Making a rapid half-turn right, on the left toe (thus turning left shoulder to partner), he repeats the same actions, namely, 1 slow right reprise and 3 side-leaps (r.l.r.). The remaining 8 bars are devoted to the left circle in broken-sequences with a cadenza on the final chord. The lady performs the same variation.

CONCLUDING PASSEGGIO

The dancers approach each other with 4 broken-sequences, swerving to left and right, and arranging to meet in the centre. This occupies the first 8 bars. The man takes the lady's right hand in his own, and they revolve to the right with 4 gliding-sequences of 2 bars each. This brings us to the end of the strain. The partners now have to regain their original positions, as at the opening of the dance, but advanced a little further forward. They will accomplish this by means of 4 more gliding-sequences, with which, releasing hands, they make their way each to the correct side of the stage (the lady passing in front of the man, from the point of view of the audience). They thus describe a semicircle, the man turning to his left, and the lady to her right. This occupies the first half of the repeat. They are now facing forward, with the lady on the man's right. Turning face to face, they perform the Grand Reverence. This occupies the remaining 8 bars of the repeat. During the final chord, they face the onlookers fully and, hand in hand, perform a short parting reverence for which the chord should be drawn out in arpeggio.

The order of the steps of Il Canario (Caroso)

Opening Passeggio

Medium reverence (riverenza minima)	4 bars
2 continenzas l.r.	4 bars
4 broken-sequences, advancing	8 bars
4 broken-sequences, revolving right	8 bars
4 broken-sequences, separating	8 bars
Cadenza (on final chord)	

First variation

8 beaten-sequences, advancing	8 bars
4 diminished reprises l.l.r.r., facing partner	8 bars
4 slow steps, retreating	8 bars
4 broken-sequences, circling left	8 bars
Cadenza on chord.	

The Canaries

Second variation

8 beaten-sequences, 2 per foot advancing	8 bars
3 minim reprises, 1 side-leap l.	4 bars
3 minim reprises, 1 side-leap r.	4 bars
3 minim reprises, 1 side-leap l.	4 bars
3 minim reprises, 1 side-leap r.	4 bars
4 broken-sequences, circling left	8 bars
Cadenza on chord.	

Intermediate passeggio

4 broken-sequences, advancing	8 bars
4 broken-sequences, revolving right	8 bars
4 broken-sequences, changing places	8 bars
4 broken-sequences, circling left	8 bars
Cadenza on chord.	

Third variation
Turn left shoulder to partner

2 beaten-sequences l.l.	2 bars
3 stamps r.l.r.; 1 beaten-sequence l.	2 bars

Turn right shoulder

2 beaten-sequences r.r.	2 bars
3 stamps l.r.l.; 1 beaten-sequence r.	2 bars

Turn left shoulder

2 beaten-sequences l.l.	2 bars
3 stamps r.l.r.; 1 beaten-sequence l.	2 bars

Turn right shoulder

2 beaten-sequences r.r.	2 bars
3 stamps l.r.l.; 1 beaten-sequence r.	2 bars
Retreat. Follow zigzag path.	
2 sliding steps, retreating sideways l.r.	2 bars
1 broken-sequence, retreating sideways l.	2 bars
2 sliding steps, retreating sideways r.l.	2 bars
1 broken-sequence, retreating sideways r.	2 bars
4 broken-sequences, circling left	8 bars
Cadenza on chord.	

The Canaries

Fourth variation

Turn left shoulder to partner

{ 8 heel-and-toe slides; 1 stamp l.	4 bars
{ 3 beaten-sequences r.l.r.; 2 stamps l.r.	4 bars

Turn right shoulder

{ 8 heel-and-toe slides; 1 stamp r.	4 bars
{ 3 beaten-sequences l.r.l.; 2 stamps	4 bars
Retreat. Keep right shoulder to partner.	
1 slow reprise l.; 3 side-leaps l.r.l.	4 bars

Turn left shoulder

1 slow reprise r.; 3 side-leaps r.l.r.	4 bars
4 broken-sequences, circling left	8 bars
Cadenza on chord.	

Concluding passeggio

4 broken-sequences, advancing towards centre	8 bars
4 gliding-sequences (scorsi), revolving right	8 bars
4 gliding-sequences, separating and	
approaching back stage	8 bars
Grand Reverence	8 bars
Short reverence to onlookers on final chord.	

HOW TO PERFORM THE STEPS

Medium reverence: This occupies 4 bars. During the first bar, stand with the weight resting on the right foot and the left foot advancing a few inches, with straightened knee and toe well pointed. At the second bar, draw back the left foot, inclining the head and body. At the third bar bend both knees a little outwards. At the fourth bar, rising on the toes, join up the left foot to the right, in the first position, and on the third beat of the bar, sink the heels. Move the free arm inward and upward and then downward and outward, marking the last two bars with wrist movements. The pair of continenzas is performed as in the preceding set of *Canaries* by Cesare Negri.

The sliding broken-sequence: The broken-sequence as used in the *Canaries* differs from that belonging to other kinds of dances, and is styled by Caroso and Negri 'seguito spezzato schisciato al Canario', i.e. the sliding broken-sequence of the *Canaries*. Caroso keeps it smooth; but Negri allows a little hop at the close. Each step occupies 2 bars of triple time. On the first beat of the first bar, slide the left foot forward on the flat of the foot, so that the heel comes level with the right toe. On the third beat, rising on the toes, slide the right toe forward so that it comes level with the middle of the left foot. On the first beat of the second bar, bending the knees slightly, slide the left foot forward on the flat of the foot till it advances a little way beyond the right toe (according to the amount of space to be covered). On the third beat of the second bar, rise on the toes. Thus you will produce a smoothly undulating effect, similar to that of the saltarello step, except that the feet never leave the ground. The right broken-sequence is performed in similar fashion, beginning with the right foot. The last broken-sequence which closes each figure of the dance ends with 2 half-steps on the toes (l.r.), made presto on the last beat, and followed by a left cadenza on the final chord.

The cadenza: This is a moderately high jump employed as a close to a series of steps. In the *Canaries* the left cadenza is used at the termination of each double strain. Standing in the fourth position right, scoop the left foot forward, simultaneously rising in the air. Then, drawing the left foot rapidly back, land precisely on the beat in the third, or the fourth position right. The third position has a neater appearance for the lady. On landing, bend the knees outward and then straighten them, rising on the toes. The preliminary movements of the cadenza are made rapidly, just in advance of the beat.

The beaten-sequence (seguito battuto): This is a step peculiar to the *Canaries*. Each sequence occupies 1 bar only. Standing on the right foot, raise the left toe and scoop the heel forward half a foot's length. This occupies the first beat. On the second beat, lowering the toe and raising the heel, slide the toe backward the same distance. On the third beat, advancing the foot again, stamp on the flat of the foot, either beside the right or in advance of it, according to whether one remains stationary or requires to move forward. Perform the right beaten-sequence in similar fashion, using the right foot. The arms should be held downwards slightly curved away from the body, with the hands half closed and the head turned towards the moving foot.

The diminished reprise (ripresa minuita): This kind of reprise is performed as previously explained in the preceding version of the *Canaries*, by Negri. Each reprise occupies 2 bars.

Slow sliding steps in retreat (passi gravi schisciati indietro): These steps occupy 2 bars each. On the first beat of bar one, slide back the left foot a foot's length behind the right, drawing back the arms (bent at the elbow) towards the left, with the body turning obliquely leftward and the head turned towards partner. At the second bar, slightly lift, and instantly replace the right toe pointed forward with no weight resting on it. Hold the right knee well straightened. This gesture serves to emphasize the rhythm in a graceful manner.

The minim reprise (ripresa minima): This type of reprise is favoured by Caroso, and is very effective when deftly performed with the body held upright and motionless, and the head erect. Each reprise occupies 1 bar and the movement is sideways. To make a left minim reprise, stand with the feet distant one inch from each other, placing the left foot about two inches in advance of the right. On the first beat raise both heels slightly and move them towards the left. On the third beat, raise the toes and move them to the left beyond the heels. This constitutes one minim reprise. Make 3 of these, to be followed by a side-leap. As you retreat sideways from your partner in this fashion, hold the arms in the opposite direction from that in which you are moving, turning your head towards your partner, as though taking leave. Perform the right minim reprise in similar fashion, but carrying the right foot two inches in advance of the left and moving towards the right.

The side-leaps (trabuchetti): These are performed as in the preceding example of the *Canaries*, described by Negri.

Medium sliding steps (passi minimi schisciati) retreating sideways: These occupy 1 bar each. In sliding the left foot in a sideways retreat, turn obliquely leftwards and for the right sliding step turn obliquely towards the right. In this zigzag fashion you will not recede too far. The same precaution applies to the sideways broken-sequence which follows the two medium sliding steps.

Sideways broken-sequence (seguito spezzato fiancheggiato): On the first beat of the first bar, slide the left foot sideways a few inches, on the flat of the foot. On the third beat of the first bar, rising on the toes, join the right foot to the left. On the first beat of the second bar, sinking the heels and bending the knees slightly, slide the left foot again leftwards. On the third beat of the second bar, rise on the toes. Make the right sideways broken-sequence in similar fashion.

The heel-and-toe steps: These consist of 3 scooping slides in a straight line, *forward, back* and *forward* (first bar), 1 slow and 1 quick slide, *backward, forward* (second bar), 2 cross-foot slides, and 1 straight, *back, forward, back* (third bar), followed by a stamp beside the stationary foot (fourth bar). The whole series of slides is first performed by the left foot and is repeated by the right in the second half of the strain. Hold the arms in the direction of the stationary foot and turn the head towards the sliding foot.

Beaten-sequences in the fourth variation, facing sideways: While performing these, the dancer should turn the head towards partner, holding the arms in the opposite direction. In making the 2 quick stamps which round off the third beaten-sequence, the first stamp should be accompanied by a vivacious leap towards partner, and the second stamp by the joining up of the other foot, in quick succession. Emphasize the leap by raising the elbow on that side, like a guard.

Slow reprise (ripresa grave) in sideways retreat: This occupies 1 bar. In making the left reprise, turn the right shoulder to partner, and on the first beat, step sideways on the flat of the foot, with bent knee. On the third beat, join up the right foot, rising on the toes. The head and arms should be turned towards partner.

Grand Reverence (riverenza grave): This ceremonial salutation closes the last passeggio, and occupies 8 bars. The partners turn face to face with the weight resting on the right foot, and with the left foot advanced a few inches. They remain thus during the first and second bars. During the third and fourth bars they draw back the left foot till the toe comes level with the right heel, inclining the head and body. During the fifth and sixth bars, the knees are bent outwards; and during the seventh and eighth bars the left foot is joined to the right in the first position, the dancers standing once more erect and rising on the toes, but sinking the heels at the close. They turn to face the audience and hand in hand perform a short reverence on the final chord. This parting reverence is performed with the same actions as the Grand Reverence but in a quarter of the time, the scope of the actions being correspondingly reduced.

The arm movements: The left hand in the Grand Reverence should be drawn inward and upward; then slowly moved downward and outward, and finally drawn inward and upward. In the short reverence the gestures are reduced, and the lady, whose left hand is held in her partner's right, performs them with her right hand.

The scorsi: These consist of little half-steps made on the tips of the toes, 2 to the beat.

The Canaries

IL CANARIO (FABRITIO CAROSO)

73

CHAPTER VI

Four Dances of Spanish Origin: Spagnoletto, Villanos, Pavaniglia (Spanish Pavan), Hachas (Torch Dance)

LO SPAGNOLETTO (CESARE NEGRI)

L O SPAGNOLETTO, as presented to us by Cesare Negri, bears the character of a Spanish rustic dance, whose vivacity accords well with its charming tune. The Spanish name of this type of dance is *Espanoletas*, but we will keep to Negri's italianized name for this particular example. Negri, who maintained his school of dancing in Milan, under Spanish domination, for half a century, may be accounted as a reliable authority on popular and court dances of Spanish origin, belonging to this period (1550–1604).

Lo Spagnoletto is set out for four dancers and is divided into three strains of 8 bars each in duple time. It contains 5 figures, all of which close with the same formula.

FIGURE I

The two couples form a quadrangle, one dancer standing at each corner, and each lady on her partner's right. Thus the two ladies face each other, standing at diagonally opposite corners, and the two men likewise. An odd half-beat at the beginning serves as a signal that the dance is about to begin. It opens with a short hopped reverence (*riverenza breve in saltino*) of 2 bars' length. This is followed by a broken double (l.) which occupies another 2 bars (advancing towards the centre) so that lady faces lady and man faces man. During the fifth and sixth bars (still converged towards the centre) they perform 2 hopped flourishes in retreat (r.l.). Then all revolve to the left (each turning on his own axis), with 1 broken double (r.). This completes the first strain. During the first 2 bars of the second strain, forming a ring, but without holding hands, the dancers circle to the left with a triple underfoot reprise, occupying 1 bar and a half, the remaining half-bar being completed by a left cadenza and a rapid right side-leap. The dancers then revolve indepen-

74

dently (each on his own axis) with a left broken double, turning to the left. This brings us to the half of the second strain. During the second half of the strain, the same actions are repeated, circling and revolving to the right; so that the dancers return to their original positions. During the first 2 bars of the third strain, they make a sideways retreat (corner-wise) by means of 2 slow steps (l.r.), fairly large, turning alternately to left and right. This is followed by a left broken double advancing towards the centre. This occupies the first half of the third strain. During the second half of the strain they again retreat (cornerwise) with 2 slow steps (r.l.), turning to right and left. The last 2 bars are occupied by a right broken double advancing, by means of which the dancers should return to their original positions, one at each corner of the quadrangle and facing towards the centre. All the doubles used in this dance are broken doubles; I will therefore omit the qualifying adjective in describing the remaining figures.

FIGURE II

Next comes the ladies' figure, during which their partners stand at ease. During the first 4 bars, they advance towards each other with 2 slow steps (l.r.) and 1 double (l.). This is followed by 2 hopped flourishes in retreat (r.l.) and another double revolving to the right, which brings them back to their original positions and completes the first strain. During the second strain they perform the triple underfoot reprise terminating with a left cadenza and rapid right side-leap; but this time, instead of circling, they travel directly sideways towards left and right, facing each other. This is followed by a left double revolving to the left. During the second half of the strain, the same actions are repeated, beginning with the right foot and moving and revolving to the right. The third strain constitutes a kind of chorus in which all four dancers join, performing the sideways retreating steps and the doubles as described in the directions for the opening figure.

The ladies now stand at ease while the men repeat the same figure, all however joining together for the chorus during the third strain, with retreating steps and doubles.

FIGURE III

In this figure all four dancers take part throughout. During the first strain they perform 2 hopped flourishes (l.r.) and 1 double, advancing, followed by 2 hopped flourishes in retreat (r.l.) and a double (r.) revolving leftward. This completes the first strain. For the second strain the dancers form a ring and circle to the left with a triple underfoot reprise as in figure I, completed by a left cadenza and rapid right side-leap. During the third and fourth bars, the dancers revolve leftwards, spinning round with a left double. This brings us to the half of the strain. During the second half they repeat the same actions, beginning with the right foot and circling and revolving to the right. The third strain is filled by the retreating steps and advancing doubles as before described.

FIGURE IV

This is a ladies' figure which is afterwards repeated by the men. During the first and second bars, turning the right shoulder towards centre, they make 2 sideways steps to the left (l.r.); the right step, which comes level with the left heel (third position left), is completed by a rapid left side-leap. During the third and fourth bars, making a quarter-turn right on the left toe, they advance towards centre with a right double. For the second half of the strain, making a quarter-turn right on the left toe, so as to have the left shoulder turned towards centre, they repeat the same actions, beginning with the right foot. After the 2 side-steps (r.l.) and right side-leap, a quarter turn left should be made on the right toe in preparation for the advancing left double. This brings us to the end of the first strain. During the first half of the second strain, the two ladies follow a semicircular path into each other's places, with a triple underfoot reprise, cadenza and side-leap, followed by a left double revolving left. Then, turning back to back, they describe another half-circle with the right underfoot reprises, etc., after which the revolving right double completes the strain and brings them once more to their original places. The third strain is danced by all four dancers, who make the retreating steps and advancing doubles as before described. The men repeat the same figure in turn, and all four dancers join in the third strain.

FIGURE V

This closing figure is performed by both couples simultaneously. To begin with, the partners link right arms and revolve to the right, with 2 hopped flourishes and 1 left double. They then release arms and each man turns towards the lady on his left. Linking left arms, he revolves with her to the left, performing the same set of steps, but beginning with the right foot. Returning to their original positions, they form a ring and circle to the left, during the second strain, with a triple underfoot reprise ending with a left cadenza and right side-leap, followed by a left double revolving to the left. This brings us to the half of the strain. During the second half, they perform the same actions, circling to the right and beginning with the right foot. The third strain is danced as in the preceding figures. At the close of the strain, the dancers perform a reverence on a final chord.

Four Dances of Spanish Origin: Spagnoletto, Villanos, Pavaniglia, Hachas

The order of the steps

FIGURE I

Hopped reverence (riverenza breve in saltino)	2 bars
1 broken double l. (seguito semidoppio)	2 bars
2 hopped flourishes r.l. (fioretti spezzati)	2 bars
1 broken double r., revolving left	2 bars
	8 bars

Triple reprise l.; cadenza l.; side-leap r.	2 bars
1 double l., revolving left	2 bars
Triple reprise r.; cadenza r.; side-leap l.	2 bars
1 double r., revolving right	2 bars
	8 bars

2 slow steps l.r., retreating	2 bars
1 double l., advancing towards centre	2 bars
2 slow steps r.l., retreating	2 bars
1 double r., advancing	2 bars
	8 bars

FIGURE II (ladies)

2 slow steps l.r. (passi gravi), advancing	2 bars
1 double l., advancing	2 bars
2 hopped flourishes r.l., retreating	2 bars
1 double r., revolving right	2 bars
	8 bars

Triple reprise l.; cadenza l.; side-leap r.	2 bars
1 double l., revolving left	2 bars
Triple reprise r.; cadenza r.; side-leap l.	2 bars
1 double r., revolving right	2 bars
	8 bars

2 slow steps l.r., retreating	2 bars
1 double l., advancing towards centre	2 bars
2 slow steps r.l., retreating	2 bars
1 double r., advancing	2 bars
	8 bars

Men repeat same figure

FIGURE III *(all together)*

2 hopped flourishes l.r., advancing	2 bars
1 double l., advancing	2 bars
2 hopped flourishes r.l., retreating	2 bars
1 double r., revolving left	2 bars
	8 bars
Triple reprise l.; cadenza l.; side-leap r.	2 bars
1 double l., revolving left	2 bars
Triple reprise r.; cadenza r.; side-leap l.	2 bars
1 double r., revolving right	2 bars
	8 bars
Third strain as in preceding figures	8 bars

FIGURE IV *(ladies)*

(Right shoulder towards centre)	
2 sideways steps l.r.; 1 left leap, presto	2 bars
Quarter-turn right; 1 double r., advancing	2 bars
(Left shoulder towards centre)	
2 sideways steps r.l.; 1 right leap, presto	2 bars
Quarter-turn left; 1 double l., advancing	2 bars
	8 bars
(Half-circle leftwards, changing places)	
Triple reprise l.; cadenza; side-leap r.	2 bars
1 double l., revolving left	2 bars

(Facing outwards, they complete circle to own places)

Triple reprise r.; cadenza r.; side-leap l.	2 bars
1 double r., revolving right	2 bars
	8 bars

Men repeat same figure

FIGURE V (*all together*)

(Couples link right arms)

2 hopped flourishes l.r.; 1 double l., revolving right	4 bars
(Men link left arms with lady on their left)	
2 hopped flourishes r.l.; 1 double r., revolving left	4 bars
	8 bars

Triple reprise l.; cadenza l.; side-leap r.	2 bars
1 double l., revolving left	2 bars
Triple reprise r.; cadenza r.; side-leap l.	2 bars
1 double r., revolving right	2 bars
	8 bars

Third strain as in preceding figures	8 bars

Short reverence on final chord.

HOW TO PERFORM THE STEPS

Short hopped reverence: At the opening of the first bar, stand on the right foot, with the left foot advanced a few inches, and at the half-bar, draw back the left foot so that the toe is level with the right heel, inclining the head and shoulders. On the first beat of the second bar, bend the knees outwards. Follow this with a little jump so as to land precisely at the half-bar, with feet joined in the first position and head and body erect.

Broken double: This kind of double is used throughout the dance and occupies 2 bars. On the first beat of bar one, step forward on the left toe, and on the third beat, step forward on the right toe. On the first beat of the second bar, step forward firmly on to the flat of the left foot, and on the second beat bring the tip of the right toe just behind the left heel, rising on the toes of both feet. On the third beat, advance the left foot about two inches, stepping on the flat of the foot and resting all the weight upon it, so that the right is just held lightly poised ready to make the next step. This type of double is of a lively character. The right double is made in similar fashion, beginning with the right foot.

Four Dances of Spanish Origin: Spagnoletto, Villanos, Pavaniglia, Hachas

The hopped flourish: Each flourish occupies 1 bar. It may be made stationary or advancing or retreating. To make a *stationary* left flourish, hop on the right toe, holding the left foot raised forward a few inches from the ground. At the second beat, lower the left toe, and touch the ground beside the right heel: on the third beat, hop on the left toe (level with the right toe) and raise the right foot forward a few inches from the ground. To make an *advancing* left flourish, hop on right toe, with the left foot raised forward: at the second beat, lower the left toe beside the right: on the third beat, hop on the left toe a few inches in advance of the right, raising the right foot forward. For a *retreating* left flourish, when lowering the left toe, at the second beat, touch the ground behind the right heel, and in making the final hop on the left toe, bring it down level with the right heel, simultaneously raising the right foot forward. The right flourish is made in similar fashion, using reverse feet.

Triple underfoot reprise (ripresa in sottopiede): This occupies 2 bars. To start the left reprise, stand on the right foot, with the left foot raised forward. On the first beat of bar one, spring sideways on to the left foot, simultaneously raising the right foot backward. On the second beat, insert the right toe beneath the left heel, projecting the left foot forward. On the third beat, spring sideways again on to the left foot, raising the right foot backward, and on the fourth beat, insert the right toe beneath the left heel, projecting the left foot forward. During the first and second beats of bar two perform once more the same actions. You will now be standing on the right foot, with the left raised forward: make a little jump, landing precisely on the third beat, with feet joined in the first position. This is a left cadenza. On the fourth beat of bar two, make a quick side-leap (*trabuchetto*) to the right, landing on the right toe with the left foot raised forward and crossing slightly in front of the right. Both knees should be well straightened. The right reprise is made in the same manner, using reverse feet and travelling towards the right.

The slow steps (passi gravi): These take 1 bar each and should be performed with a suave dignity. On the first beat, step forward or backward, as may be required, on the flat of the foot, and at the half-bar, rise a little on the toes, swaying the body slightly towards the side of the stepping foot.

Broken doubles revolving: When making the first little step on the toe, execute, simultaneously, a half-turn on it to left or right according to the direction in which you are turning. With the second little step, make another half-turn so as to complete the revolution. On the first beat of the second bar, step forward on the flat of the foot, and on the second beat bring the toe of the backward foot up to the heel of the forward one, rising on the toes. On the third beat, advance the front foot two inches, treading on the flat of the foot. The type of double used throughout this dance is termed by Negri *seguito ordinario*, whereas Caroso names it *seguito semidoppio*, applying the qualification *ordinario* to another, less ornate kind of step. To avoid confusion I have therefore translated Negri's *seguito ordinario* as 'broken double', with whose movements it coincides.

Short concluding reverence: Make this in the same manner as the opening reverence, but,

80

instead of hopping on the last beat, merely rise on the toes and sink the heels at the close.

The arm movements: These are moderate and mostly done from the forearm, or the wrist only. In the revolving movements the arms can move more vigorously, to give impetus to the turn. As the dancer faces forward after the turn, the arms can move downward and outward with a curving motion. At the start of the hopped flourish, the arms should be held in the opposite direction from that of the raised foot, while the head turns in the reverse direction from that of the arms. Towards the close of the flourish, the arms move to the other side, in preparation for the succeeding flourish, and the head turns towards the newly raised foot.

For the underfoot reprises, the arms point in the opposite direction from that in which the dancer is travelling. On landing from the cadenza, draw the arms downward and outward; and with the ensuing side-leap move them to the opposite side from that towards which you are leaping, keeping the upper arm low. The slow steps should be accompanied by a slight movement of the forearm and hand towards the side of the stepping foot. When you make these steps in retreat the arm movements are more marked, and are made in the direction of the stepping foot. During the short reverence, move the arms inward and upward and then downward and outward with moderation, finishing with a turn of the wrist.

LO SPAGNOLETTO (CESARE NEGRI)

Chord to
conclude
the dance

VILLANOS (CESARE NEGRI)

This is a Spanish dance of rustic character which Cesare Negri (employing an unusual Italian diminutive) entitles *Villanicco*. The Italian masters sometimes used a diminutive termination for dances whose steps were diminished, i.e. cut up into quicker steps, as witness the title *Pavaniglia*, applied to the Spanish *Pavan*. Negri's version of *Villanos* is set out for four dancers, but he tells us that, as the dance is of a cheerful and convivial nature, the number of dancers may be multiplied at pleasure. It has six figures, the third figure being performed twice over; that is to say, first by the men alone, and then by the ladies. If it is desired to increase the number of dancers, eight will form a satisfactory ensemble.

VILLANOS

Four Dances of Spanish Origin: Spagnoletto, Villanos, Pavaniglia, Hachas

FIGURE I

The four dancers stand, one at each corner of the quadrangle, with the ladies on the right of their partners. The music for figure I consists of one strain of 4 bars (duple time) which is repeated, making 8 bars in all. The dance opens with a reverence during which the partners, standing cornerwise, and facing towards the centre, are turned obliquely towards each other. The reverence occupies 2 bars, and is followed by 2 broken doubles (*seguiti semidoppi*) of 1 bar each, during which the dancers revolve to the left, each turning independently on his own axis. During the fifth and sixth bars, facing once more towards the centre, they advance with 1 broken double (l.) which is followed by 4 stationary hopped steps (r.l.r.l.), raising the other foot forward as though marking time. The seventh bar is occupied by 2 hopped flourishes in retreat (r.l.) and the eighth bar with a right broken double revolving to the right. This brings the dancers back to their original positions at each corner of the quadrangle.

As all the doubles used in this dance are of the broken variety, I will henceforth omit the qualifying adjective.

FIGURE II

This strain consists of 4 bars repeated, making 8 bars in all. The dancers form a ring facing outwards, all linking arms (by the forearm). During the first 4 bars they circle leftwards by means of 4 doubles (l.r.l.r.). They separate and make a half-turn left on the right toe, so as to face centre. During the fifth bar they revolve to the left with 1 double (l.), returning to their places facing inward.

The sixth bar is occupied by 4 stationary hopped steps (r.l.r.l.), raising the other foot forward, and the seventh bar by 2 hopped flourishes in retreat (r.l.). During the eighth bar, they revolve to the right, with a right double. This brings them back to their original positions at each corner of the quadrangle.

FIGURE III

This figure occupies 8 bars, and is first performed by the men alone. At the repeat of the strain the ladies perform the identical figure in their turn, while the men remain stationary. During the first 2 bars the two dancers concerned advance towards each other with 2 slow steps (l.r.) and 1 left double. This is followed by 2 dotted singles in retreat (r.l.) occupying 1 bar, and 2 quick continenzas (r.l.) taking half a bar each, which brings us to the end of the fourth bar. During the fifth bar (turning the right shoulder towards centre), they make a right diminished reprise. At the sixth bar, they make a rapid quarter-turn right, on the right toe, so as to come face to face in the centre, and perform 4 stationary hops. The seventh bar is occupied by 2 hopped flourishes in retreat (r.l.) and the eighth bar by a right double revolving to the right as in the preceding figures, thus regaining their original positions at the corners of the quadrangle.

FIGURE IV

The partners turn to face each other directly and both couples, linking their right arms, revolve to the right with 2 doubles. This occupies 2 bars. Releasing their hold with a slight inclination, all four dancers revolve independently to the left on their own axis with 2 more doubles (l.r.), returning to their original positions. The partners turn to face each other again and, during the fifth and sixth bars, perform 2 diminished reprises (l.r.) in contrary motion. With a rapid quarter-turn (man left and lady right), they once more face towards centre and, during the seventh bar, make 2 hopped flourishes (r.l.). During the eighth bar they revolve to the right, with 1 right double, thus regaining their original positions.

For the repeat of this 8-bar strain, the two men, relinquishing their own partners, turn each towards the lady on their other side. Linking left arms, the couples revolve to the left with 2 doubles (r.l.). Releasing their hold with a slight inclination, all four dancers (turning independently) revolve to the right with 2 more doubles (r.l.). During the fifth and sixth bars, turning face to face, they perform 2 diminished reprises in contrary motion (r.l.). This is followed by 2 hopped flourishes facing towards centre (r.l.) and 1 double (r.), revolving to the right, thus regaining their original positions.

FIGURE V

This strain consists of 4 bars repeated, making 8 bars in all. The dancers form a ring, facing outwards and linking their forearms as in figure II. During the first 4 bars, they circle leftwards with 4 sideways doubles. Releasing their hold, they make a rapid half-turn left on the right toe, thus facing towards centre. During the fifth and sixth bars, they revolve to the left, on their own axis, with 2 slow steps (l.r.) and 1 double (l.). During the seventh and eighth bars, they revolve similarly to the right, with 2 slow steps (r.l.) and 1 double (r.), regaining their respective positions at each corner at the close.

FIGURE VI

Finale

This figure occupies a strain of 8 bars and is an exact repetition of figure III, except that this time all four dancers dance simultaneously. At the close of the strain a chord is played in arpeggio, during which the dancers, standing at each corner of the quadrangle, and facing towards centre, make a short reverence.

Four Dances of Spanish Origin: Spagnoletto, Villanos, Pavaniglia, Hachas

The order of the steps

FIGURE I

First strain with repeat:

Reverence	2 bars
2 broken doubles, revolving left, l.r.	2 bars
1 broken double, advancing l.; 4 hops, r.l.r.l.	2 bars
2 flourishes r.l., retreating; one double r., revolving right	2 bars
	8 bars

FIGURE II

Second strain with repeat:

Form ring facing outwards

4 doubles, circling left; (release) half-turn left	4 bars
1 left double, revolving left; 4 hops r.l.r.l.	2 bars
2 flourishes r.l.; one double r., revolving right	2 bars
	8 bars

FIGURE III

Third strain:

First time men only: second time ladies

2 slow steps l.r.; one double l., advancing	2 bars
2 dotted singles (retreating) r.l.; 2 continenzas r.l.	2 bars
1 diminished reprise r.; 4 hops r.l.r.l.	2 bars
2 hopped flourishes r.l.; one double r., revolving right	2 bars
	8 bars

(Ladies repeat same)

FIGURE IV

Fourth strain:
    Partners link right arms

2 doubles l.r., revolving right	2 bars
Release arms	
2 doubles l.r., revolving left	2 bars
2 diminished reprises l.r.	2 bars
2 hopped flourishes r.l.; 1 right double, revolving r.	2 bars
Change partners and link left arms	
2 doubles r.l., revolving left	2 bars
Release arms	
2 doubles r.l., revolving right	2 bars
2 diminished reprises r.l.	2 bars
2 hopped flourishes r.l.; one left double, revolving r.	2 bars
	16 bars

FIGURE V

Fifth strain:
    Form ring facing outwards

4 doubles circling left; (release) half-turn l.	4 bars
2 slow steps l.r.; 1 left double, revolving l.	2 bars
2 slow steps r.l.; 1 right double, revolving r.	2 bars
	8 bars

FIGURE VI

Sixth strain:

Finale

2 slow steps l.r.; 1 double l., advancing	2 bars
Dotted single (retreating) r.l.; 2 continenzas r.l.	2 bars
1 diminished reprise r.; 4 hops r.l.r.l.	2 bars
2 hopped flourishes r.l.; right double, revolving r.	2 bars
	8 bars

Short reverence.

Final chord

HOW TO PERFORM THE STEPS

Medium reverence: This occupies 2 bars. Standing on the right foot with the left foot advanced a few inches, remain thus during the first and second beats of bar one. At the half-bar, draw back the left foot so that the toe comes level with the right heel and gently incline the head and body. During the first half of bar two, bend the knees a little outward and then, throwing the weight on the left foot, straighten the right knee. On the third beat, restore the weight on to the right foot and simultaneously join the left foot to it, rising on to the toes, and straightening the head and body. Sink the heels at the close.

The broken double: This is performed in 1 bar of 4 beats. On the first beat, step forward lightly on the left toe, and on the second beat, make a similar step on the right toe. On the third beat, step forward firmly on the flat of the left foot, and at the half-beat, bring up the tip of the right toe just behind the left heel, rising on the toes. On the fourth beat advance the left foot about two inches, treading on the flat of the foot and resting all the weight upon it, so that the right foot is held lightly poised on the toe, ready to begin the right double.

Broken double, revolving: When making the first 2 steps on the toes, execute about one-third of a turn on each. On the third beat, step on the flat of the foot, and as you subsequently rise on the toes, make another third of a turn, to complete the revolution. The remainder of the double is performed facing towards the centre of the quadrangle. Where 2 broken doubles are employed in the revolution, make your circle a little wider and the turns on each toe rather smaller.

The 4 hops: One hop goes to each beat, and is accompanied by the raising of the other foot forward with well-pointed toe.

The double in outward circle: When the dancers face outward for their leftward circling, with linked arms, make the left double as follows. Start on the first beat with a sideways step on the left toe. On the second beat, make a leftward sideways step on the right toe behind the left foot, so that the right toe lands on the *outside* of the left heel. On the third beat, step again sideways with the left foot, but this time on the flat of the foot. At the half-beat, rising on the toes, bring the right toe level with the *inside* of the left heel (fifth position left); and on the fourth beat, step again sideways on the flat of the left foot, but rising again on the toes at the half-beat. This is followed by a right double still circling leftward, as follows. On the first beat, step leftwards on the right toe behind the left foot, placing the right toe by the *outside* of the left heel. On the second beat, step sideways with the left toe, passing in front of the right. On the third beat, step leftwards on the flat of the right foot, passing it behind the left, so as to land beyond the left heel. At the half-beat, rising on the toes, make a little step leftwards on the left toe, so as to land in the fifth position left; and on the fourth beat, step again leftwards on the flat of the right foot behind the left, landing a little beyond the left heel. This completes the right broken double, circling leftwards. Follow on with a second left and a second right double, as described above, so as to complete your leftward circle facing outward.

The hopped flourish: In *Villanos* all the flourishes are made in retreat. To make a right flourish, hop on the left toe, holding the right foot raised forward a few inches from the ground. At the half-beat, lower the right toe behind the left heel. On the second beat, hop on the right foot (landing on the ball of the foot behind the left heel) and raise the left foot forward ready for the left flourish. According to the arrangement of the steps in this dance, wherever there occurs a pair of flourishes it is the right flourish which comes first.

The slow steps: These occupy half a bar each. Step forward a few inches on the flat of the left foot, swaying a little in that direction and rising on the toes on the second beat. Follow with the right slow step in similar fashion during the third and fourth beats.

The quick continenzas: These occupy 1 bar together. On the first beat of bar one, extend the right foot sideways a few inches, bending both knees outwards. At the second beat, join the left foot to the right in the first position, rising on the toes. Perform the left continenza in similar fashion, moving towards the left, during the third and fourth beats.

The dotted singles: These occupy 1 bar together. On the first beat, step backward on the flat of the right foot, and, just after the second beat, join the left foot to it, rising on the toes. Perform the left single in similar fashion during the third and fourth beats. Turn the body first obliquely towards the right, and then towards the left, retreating in zigzag movement.

The arm movements: The reverence should be accompanied by graceful gestures. If the man is in historical costume, and consequently wearing a hat, he should proceed as follows. During the first half of bar one, he raises his left hand to his hat and grasps it by the brim: during the second half of the bar, he removes it with a downward and outward movement of the arm, keeping the inside turned towards himself. Raising it again with the same curving movements of the arm during the first half of bar two, he replaces it firmly on his head, and in the closing half-bar once again lowers the arm in an outward direction. The gestures of the lady are more simple, consisting of the slow movement of the right hand and forearm inward and upward during the first bar and downward and outward during the second. Should the man not be wearing a hat, he may make the same gestures as those of the lady, but using the left hand.

When making the left broken double advancing, the dancer should accompany the first 2 steps with a slight movement of the left hand to left and right, the broken step which follows these being emphasized by a wider movement of the forearm leftwards. The other arm should be bent a little outwards, and drawn inward again in preparation for the movements with which it should accompany the right broken double which follows. In a revolving double, it is the outside arm which gives the necessary impetus to the swift turn; but the other arm moves a little outward at the close, for symmetry of pose.

Four Dances of Spanish Origin: *Spagnoletto, Villanos, Pavaniglia, Hachas*

In the hopped flourish, turn the head towards the side of the raised foot, and hold the arms in the opposite direction.

In the reprises (both diminished and underfoot) turn both head and arms in the opposite direction from that in which you are travelling.

For the music to accompany this dance I have chosen a Spanish *Villanos* tune of outstanding charm in place of the less interesting one supplied by Negri.

VILLANOS

1. Men's Solo figure
2. Ladies' Solo figure

PAVANIGLIA (CAROSO)

(*The Spanish Pavan*)

Cesare Negri gives us two examples of the Spanish *Pavan*, one being entitled *Pavaniglia a la Romana* and the other *Pavaniglia al modo di Milano*. A third version of this dance is supplied by Fabritio Caroso, simply entitled *Pavaniglia*. The last-named example has the advantage of having been set to the beautiful tune composed by Antonio de Cabezon (*c.* 1550). It contains 16 figures. Five of these, however, are a repetition of preceding figures, with the difference that the steps start with the opposite foot. The dance, as set out by Caroso, is for two dancers who stand hand in hand, facing the spectators to begin with, but separate towards the middle, coming together again for the conclusion. The music is in duple time with 2 minims to the bar, and goes at a lively pace, unlike the solemn processional pavan.

Four Dances of Spanish Origin: Spagnoletto, Villanos, Pavaniglia, Hachas

FIGURE I

The partners stand side by side, but turned obliquely towards each other, the lady on the man's right. He holds her left hand in his right. The music consists of a strain of 16 bars, repeated throughout the dance, each figure occupying one strain. The Grand Reverence (*riverenza grave*) opens the dance and occupies 8 bars. It is followed by a pair of medium continenzas taking 2 bars each (l.r.). As you sink the heels at the close of the second one, raise the left foot forward about two inches from the ground. At the thirteenth bar, rapidly draw back the left foot and, placing it behind the right heel, bend both knees outwards. At the half-bar, rise again on the toes. This constitutes a quick reverence (*riverenza presta*). During the fourteenth bar, hop on the right foot, and raise the left foot forward, bringing it down again at the half-bar. The Italians called this step a *zoppetto* (meaning a limping hop) and we will retain the Italian name for conciseness. During the fifteenth bar, make a stationary galliard step (r.), which Caroso names, *passo largo fermato in gagliarda*; and, during the last bar, bring the figure to a close with a right cadenza, finishing with the feet joined in the first position.

FIGURE II

All the figures of this dance, with the exception of the first, open with a series of steps which occupies the first 4 bars, and only varies in that it starts sometimes with the left foot and at other times with the right. Also the last 4 bars of each figure follow a set pattern, with the exception of those of the closing figure, which are occupied with the final salutations. Once these two sections have been memorized, there will only remain the varied passages which occupy the intervening 8 bars, to be learned by heart. During figure II, face forward, hand in hand, turning slightly towards each other, as in the opening figure. Bars one and two are occupied by a slow, left dotted single (*puntata grave*), advancing. At bar three, step forward on the flat of the right foot, simultaneously advancing the left foot, raised two inches. Then (rising on the toes of the right foot) rapidly draw back the left behind the right heel. At the half-bar, bend both knees outwards and rise again quickly. This constitutes a quick half-reverence (*mezza riverenza presta*) and completes the third bar. At the fourth bar, make a springing right underfoot step (*sotto piede*) and finish it with a right cadenza, from which you land with the right foot behind the left in the third position left.

The middle section which follows is composed of 8 hopped flourishes advancing, beginning with the right foot raised forward. The closing section of 4 bars runs as follows. On the first beat of bar thirteen, make a right cadenza, landing with the right foot behind the left in the third position left. On the first beat of bar fourteen, hopping on the left foot, make a right zoppetto. On the first beat of bar fifteen, make a galliard step (l.) (*passo in gagliarda*); and on the first beat of bar sixteen, make a right cadenza, landing with the feet joined, in the first position.

91

FIGURE III

This figure follows the pattern of the preceding one, but starts with the right foot instead of the left. The 8 hopped flourishes start with the left foot raised forward and are made in retreat (turning slightly from side to side) to compensate for the advancing passage in figure II. In the fourteenth and fifteenth bars of the strain, the lady is given the alternative of three side-leaps (*trabuchetti*) in place of the zoppetto and galliard step. As, however, the partners are still facing forward, hand in hand, I find the general appearance more symmetrical if she adheres to the same steps as those performed by the man.

FIGURE IV

In this figure the man starts with the left foot and the lady with the right. They perform the 4 opening bars still facing forward. For the middle 8-bar section, they turn face to face, though still holding hands. I will describe the variation as though performed by the man, it being understood that the lady is using the opposite foot, so that in their little side-hops and jumps they travel in the same direction. During the fifth bar, the man makes 2 little side-jumps (*balzetti*), on the toes (with the feet joined in the first position) towards the left. During bar six, he makes 2 side-kicks (*costatetti*) to left and right, simultaneously hopping on the other foot. During bar seven he makes 2 balzetti to the right and, in bar eight, 2 costatetti (r.l.). In bar nine, he makes 2 balzetti, one to the left and the other to the right; and in bar ten, 2 costatetti (l.r.). Bars eleven and twelve are occupied by 2 chasing steps (*recacciati*), with left and right foot. This concludes the intermediate variation. The partners once more face forward for the concluding 4 bars, which follow the established formula. The man starts with the left foot and the lady with the right. As the lady is credited with less agility than that of her partner, she is advised, in the middle section, to replace the costatetti with 2 side-leaps (*trabuchetti*) and the recacciati with 2 slow steps (*passi gravi*) in retreat. But again, I think it preferable for the partners, whilst holding hands, to perform identical movements. If her skirts are very long and ample she can reduce the height of the side-kicks in the costatetti, and the back-kicks in the recacciati.

FIGURE V

This is a repetition of figure IV, with the difference that the man starts with the right foot and the lady with the left. Also, in the opening and closing sections, the advancing steps are made in retreat: namely, the dotted single and slow step in the first part, and the zoppetto in the last part.

FIGURE VI

In this figure the partners face forward, hand in hand. During the first 4 bars, they perform the opening formula, both partners starting this time with the left foot. During the middle section, they continue to face forward, hand in hand, and perform the following variation: Bar five is occupied by 2 balzetti (l.r.) and bar six by an underfoot step (l.) and left cadenza. Bars seven and eight are filled with a group of 3 side-leaps (r.l.r.) and an underfoot step (l.), closing with joined feet. This group of steps is called a *groppo*. In the groppo, the foot which is raised kicks backward instead of pointing forward as in the ordinary side-leaps. This completes the first half of the variation. The second half is an exact repeat of the first half, but beginning with the right foot. The concluding 4 bars follow the established formula, namely, right cadenza and zoppetto, left galliard step and right cadenza, landing with feet joined in the first position.

FIGURE VII

This figure is an exact repetition of figure VI, but starting with the right foot so that the opposite foot, for all steps, is employed throughout.

FIGURE VIII

Facing forward, hand in hand, the partners perform the opening formula, starting with the left foot. At the close of the 4 bars, the man, kissing the lady's hand, releases it. During the intervening 8 bars they make a passeggio following independent paths. Each describes a figure S, the man (turning leftwards and moving horizontally) arrives at his original position, while the lady (turning leftwards and travelling forward) arrives at the opposite end of the dance. Face to face, they perform the closing formula. The lady may avail herself of this opportunity to make use of the alternative movements, suggested for her by Caroso, namely, 3 side-leaps and cadenza, closing with the feet joined in the first position. The man in place of the usual cadenza is told to make 2 quick cabrioles (*capriole preste*).

FIGURE IX

Standing face to face, at either end of the dance, the partners perform the opening formula, starting with the left foot. The underfoot step in bar four is terminated by the lowering of the right foot beside the left, in place of the usual cadenza. The intermediate variation proceeds as follows: In bar five, turn obliquely towards the right, and, hopping on the right foot, cross the left foot over the right knee. At the half-bar, leap sideways on to it, making a left underfoot step. At bar six, hop on the right foot (which will have been inserted beneath the left) and make a left sideways zoppetto. During bars seven and eight, turn obliquely leftwards, and repeat the actions of bars five and six, using the contrary feet throughout and moving towards the right. During bars nine and ten, turn obliquely towards the right and repeat once again the same actions as those performed in bars five and six. In bar eleven, hopping on the left foot, make 2 bell-clapper steps (*campanelle*) with the right foot. During the twelfth bar, make 2 more campanelle with the left foot, lowering it quickly at the close. The concluding 4 bars follow the established formula: namely, a right cadenza, right zoppetto, left galliard step and right cadenza, landing with the feet joined in the first position.

FIGURE X

Figure X is a repetition of figure IX, but starting with the right foot instead of the left, thus using the contrary foot throughout.

FIGURE XI

In this figure the dancers remain at opposite ends of the dance. The opening formula starts with the left foot. In the intermediate section of 8 bars, the variation allotted to the lady differs radically from that of the man. The concluding 4 bars are performed according to the usual formula. I will first describe the man's variation. At bar five, with a rapid quarter-turn left, he makes a right hopped flourish, and at bar six, an underfoot step (*sotto piede*) towards the left (without cadenza). He follows this at the half-bar (third beat) with a quick left zoppetto (hopping on the right foot, with left foot raised, and brought down on the fourth beat). At bar seven, he makes an underfoot step toward the right (without cadenza), and at the half-bar, a right side-leap (*trabuchetto*). At bar eight he makes a left side-leap, and at the half-bar, a right zoppetto. At the close of bar eight, he makes a half-turn right, presenting his left profile to partner. During the following 4 bars, he repeats the foregoing variation, starting with a left hopped flourish and using the contrary foot throughout. In this variation, Caroso had accidentally left the dancer on the wrong foot at the end of each 4 bars, which discrepancy I have remedied by substituting a second side-leap for a half-reverence in each case.

The lady's variation is suave and graceful, forming an effective contrast to that of her partner. At bar five, she makes a left side-leap, followed at the half-bar by a hop. This constitutes a trabuchetto grave. At bar six, she makes another to the right. This is followed at bar seven by a slow step forward, on the left foot. At the half-bar, rising on the toes, she advances the right foot and quickly draws it back again, placing it behind the left heel. At bar eight she makes a half-reverence, and at the half-bar (third beat), rises on the toes, sinking the heels at the fourth beat. During the remaining 4 bars, she repeats the foregoing variation, beginning with the right foot. The concluding formula starts, for both dancers, with a right cadenza landing with the right foot behind the left, followed by a right zoppetto, a left galliard step and a right cadenza, landing with the feet joined in the first position.

FIGURE XII

Figure XII is a repetition of figure XI, but starting with the right foot instead of the left, thus using the contrary foot throughout.

FIGURE XIII

This figure opens with the usual formula, starting with the left foot. The partners remain at opposite ends of the dance and again perform entirely independent variations.

Four Dances of Spanish Origin: Spagnoletto, Villanos, Pavaniglia, Hachas

I will begin by describing the man's elaborate series of steps. At the close of bar four, which ends with a right cadenza (landing with the right foot beside the left), he makes a quarter-turn left on the toes. At the fifth bar, he makes a right zoppetto, raising the right foot backwards and bringing it down at the half-bar, with the toe level with the left heel. At bar six, he makes a left feigned sequence (*seguito finto*) and, at the close of this (on the fourth beat), a half-turn right, so as to present the left profile to partner. At bar seven he makes a right feigned sequence and, at bar eight, a left zoppetto, hopping on the right foot and raising the left foot backwards. At the half-bar, the left foot is lowered so that the toe comes level with the right heel. During bar nine, he makes 3 quick steps (*passi presti*) to the right, and, on the fourth beat of the bar, a half-turn left on the right toe. During bar ten, he makes 3 quick steps to the left, and on the fourth beat of the bar, a quarter-turn right, on the left toe. During bars eleven and twelve, he makes 2 sideways flourishes (r.l.), facing partner. This completes his variation.

To the lady is allotted a less-complicated variation, which, however, when performed with fluent grace, is highly decorative. It consists of a passeggio, made entirely with gliding half-steps (*scorsi*). This is best performed so as to describe a spacious double-circle in front of partner. The dancer should start leftwards, and, having completed her first circle at the close of bar eight, make another to the right during the remaining 4 bars of her variation. The closing 4 bars of the strain are performed by both dancers according to the established formula, beginning with a right cadenza, followed by a right zoppetto (with the right foot raised forward), a left galliard step, and a right cadenza, landing with the feet joined in the first position.

FIGURE XIV

This figure is a repetition of figure XIII, but starts with the right foot, using the opposite foot throughout.

FIGURE XV

Standing face to face, the partners perform the opening formula, beginning with the left foot. The intermediate 8 bars are occupied by a passeggio of 8 hopped flourishes, starting with the right flourish (with the right foot raised forward a few inches). Both dancers advance until they meet near the centre of the dance, when the man circles towards his left, thus coming back to his starting-point. The lady meanwhile veers towards her left for 2 bars, and then, bearing to her right, curves round so as to take up her position beside the man, on his right. He takes her left hand in his own right, and, facing forward, they perform the closing formula.

FIGURE XVI

Facing forward, hand in hand, the partners perform the opening formula, starting with the *right* foot. During bars five and six, they advance with 3 slow steps (l.r.l.), the third of which comes on the first beat of bar six. At the half-bar they advance the right foot (well pointed) with no weight on it. During bars seven and eight, they retreat with 3 more slow steps (r.l.r.) and, at the half-bar of bar eight, they pause again, slightly raising and replacing the left foot in front, with no weight on it. During the remaining 8 bars of the strain, they perform the Grand Reverence, facing forward, but turned obliquely towards each other.

The Spanish Pavan constitutes an important example of the Spanish Court Dances of the Renaissance Period. Though it is here set out in its entirety, performers can shorten it at will, choosing such figures as they find most pleasing. It is best to include the first two figures and the last two, and to alternate the starting of the intermediate ones (where possible) with left and right foot for the sake of variety. Naturally in figure IV the partners, who face each other, though hand in hand, must use opposite feet.

The order of the steps

FIGURE I

Grand Reverence	8 bars
2 continenzas l.r.	4 bars
Quick reverence l. and zoppetto l. (left foot raised)	2 bars
Galliard step r.; cadenza r.	2 bars
	16 bars

FIGURE II

Dotted single (puntata grave) l.	2 bars
Slow step r. and half-reverence l.	1 bar
Underfoot step r. and right cadenza	1 bar
8 hopped flourishes advancing r.l.	8 bars
Right cadenza (landing third position l.)	1 bar
Right zoppetto (right foot raised)	1 bar
Galliard step l.	1 bar
Right cadenza (landing first position)	1 bar
	16 bars

FIGURE III

Repetition of figure II but starting with the right foot instead of the left. The 8 hopped flourishes l.r. are made in retreat.

FIGURE IV

Man and lady use opposite feet throughout. Man starts with left foot and lady with right.

Dotted single (man l., lady r.)	2 bars
Slow step (man r., lady l.); half-reverence (man l., lady r.)	1 bar
Underfoot step (man r., lady l.); cadenza	1 bar
	4 bars

Variation

Holding hands, the partners face each other.

2 balzetti (man l., lady r.)	1 bar
2 costatetti (man l.r., lady r.l.)	1 bar
2 balzetti (man r., lady l.)	1 bar
2 costatetti (man r.l., lady l.r.)	1 bar
2 balzetti (man l.r., lady r.l.)	1 bar
2 costatetti (man l.r., lady r.l.)	1 bar
2 recacciate (man l.r., lady r.l.)	2 bars
	8 bars

Facing forward

Cadenza (man l., lady r.)	1 bar
Zoppetto (man l., lady r.)	1 bar
Galliard step (man r., lady l.)	1 bar
Cadenza (man l., lady r.) landing first position	1 bar
	4 bars

FIGURE V

Repetition of figure IV, but with man starting with the right foot and lady with the left.

FIGURE VI

Partners face forward, hand in hand. Both start with the left foot.

⎧ Dotted single l.	2 bars
⎨ Slow step r. and half-reverence l.	1 bar
⎩ Underfoot step r.; cadenza r.	1 bar
	4 bars

Variation

2 balzetti l.r.	1 bar
Underfoot step l.; cadenza l.	1 bar
Groppo (3 leaps r.l.r. and chasing step)	2 bars
2 balzetti r.l.	1 bar
Underfoot step r.; cadenza r.	1 bar
Groppo (3 leaps l.r.l. and chasing step)	2 bars
	8 bars

⎧ Cadenza r.	1 bar
⎨ Zoppetto r. (right foot raised)	1 bar
⎨ Galliard step l.	1 bar
⎩ Cadenza r. (landing first position)	1 bar
	4 bars

FIGURE VII

Repetition of figure VI, but starting with the right foot.

FIGURE VIII

Partners face forward, hand in hand, and start with the left foot.

⎧ Dotted single l.	2 bars
⎨ Slow step r. and half-reverence l.	1 bar
⎩ Underfoot step r.; cadenza r.	1 bar
	4 bars

Passeggio

Partners release hands and separate.

8 hopped flourishes r.l.

8 bars

In this passeggio the man (circling left) goes to the foot of the dance (back stage), and the lady (circling left) proceeds to the head (front stage).

Closing formula

Cadenza r.	1 bar
Zoppetto r. (right foot raised)	1 bar
Galliard step l.	1 bar
Cadenza r. (landing first position)	1 bar
(Man, in place of cadenza, makes 2 cabrioles)	
	4 bars

FIGURE IX

Partners face each other at either end of the dance.

Dotted single l.	2 bars
Slow step r. and half-reverence l.	1 bar
Underfoot step r.; join feet in first position	1 bar
	4 bars

Variation

Left crossfoot and underfoot step l.	1 bar
Left zoppetto (left foot raised)	1 bar
Right crossfoot and underfoot step r.	1 bar
Right zoppetto (right foot raised)	1 bar
Left crossfoot and underfoot step l.	1 bar
Left zoppetto (left foot raised)	1 bar
2 bell-clapper steps (campanelle) r.	1 bar
2 bell-clapper steps l. (lower left foot at close)	1 bar
	8 bars

Closing formula

⌈Cadenza r.	1 bar
⎪Zoppetto r. (right foot raised)	1 bar
⎨Galliard step l.	1 bar
⎩Cadenza r. (landing first position)	1 bar
	4 bars

FIGURE X

Repetition of figure IX, but starting with the right foot.

FIGURE XI

Partners face each other at either end of the dance.

⌈Dotted single l.	2 bars
⎨Slow step r. and half-reverence l.	1 bar
⎩Underfoot step r.; cadenza r.	1 bar
	4 bars

Man's variation (quarter-turn l.)

Hopped flourish r.	1 bar
Underfoot step l.; zoppetto presto l. (left raised)	1 bar
Underfoot step r.; side-leap r.	1 bar
Side-leap l.; zoppetto presto r. (right raised)	1 bar
	4 bars

(Half-turn right)

Hopped flourish l.	1 bar
Underfoot step r.; zoppetto presto r.	1 bar
Underfoot step l.; side-leap l.	1 bar
Side-leap r.; zoppetto presto l.	1 bar
	4 bars

Lady's simultaneous variation

Side-leap l.; hop l. (right foot crossed)	1 bar
Side-leap r.; hop r. (left foot crossed)	1 bar
Slow-step l.; advance and withdraw right	1 bar
Half-reverence r.; rise on toes and sink	1 bar
Side-leap r.; hop r. (left foot crossed)	1 bar
Side-leap l.; hop l. (right foot crossed)	1 bar
Slow-step r.; advance and withdraw left	1 bar
Half-reverence l.; rise on toes and sink	1 bar
	8 bars

Closing formula

Cadenza r.	1 bar
Zoppetto r.	1 bar
Galliard step l.	1 bar
Cadenza r. (landing first position)	1 bar
	4 bars

FIGURE XII

Repetition of figure XI, but starting with the right foot. Man makes a quarter-turn right at close of opening formula, and starts variation with a left hopped flourish.

FIGURE XIII

Partners face each other at either end of the dance.

⎧ Dotted single l.	2 bars
⎨ Slow step r. and half-reverence l.	1 bar
⎩ Underfoot step r.; cadenza r.	1 bar
	4 bars

Man's variation (*quarter-turn l.*)

Zoppetto r. (right foot raised backward and lowered at half-bar)	1 bar
Left feigned sequence (half-turn right)	1 bar
Right feigned sequence	1 bar
Zoppetto l. (left foot raised backward and lowered at half-bar)	1 bar
3 quick steps r.l.r. (half-turn left)	1 bar
3 quick steps l.r.l. (quarter-turn right)	1 bar
2 sideways flourishes r.l.	2 bars
	8 bars

Lady's simultaneous variation

The lady executes 2 circles l.r. with 2 gliding-sequences of 4 bars each. Caroso describes this ornate passeggio as *una bella scorsa*   8 bars

Closing formula

Cadenza r.	1 bar
Zoppetto r.	1 bar
Galliard step l.	1 bar
Cadenza r. (landing first position)	1 bar
	4 bars

FIGURE XIV

Repetition of figure XIII, but starting with the right foot.

FIGURE XV

Dotted single l.	2 bars
Slow step r. and half-reverence l.	1 bar
Underfoot step r.; cadenza r.	1 bar
	4 bars

Passeggio

8 hopped flourishes r.l.	8 bars

Closing formula

⎧Cadenza r.	1 bar
⎪Zoppetto r.	1 bar
⎨Galliard step l.	1 bar
⎩Cadenza r. (landing first position)	1 bar
	4 bars

FIGURE XVI

⎧Dotted single r.	2 bars
⎨Slow step l. and half-reverence r.	1 bar
⎩Underfoot step l.; cadenza l.	1 bar
	4 bars

INTERMEDIATE SECTION

⎧3 slow steps advancing l.r.l.; pause, advancing right foot	2 bars
⎨3 slow steps retreating r.l.r.; pause, pointing left foot forward	2 bars
	4 bars

Finale

Grand Reverence	8 bars

HOW TO PERFORM THE STEPS

The Grand Reverence: This occupies 8 bars. Standing on the right foot, with the left foot advanced a few inches, remain thus during the first and second bars. During the third and fourth bars, draw back the left foot so that the toe comes level with the right heel, and gently incline the head and body. During bars five and six bend the knees outward slightly, and then, putting the weight wholly on the left foot, straighten the right knee and point the toe. At bar seven, restore the weight on to the right foot, and simultaneously join the left foot to it, rising on the toes and straightening the head and body. At bar eight, sink the heels.

Four Dances of Spanish Origin: Spagnoletto, Villanos, Pavaniglia, Hachas

The arm movements: If the man is in historical costume, and consequently wearing a hat, he raises his left hand during bars one and two and grasps the hat by the brim. During bars three and four, he removes it with a downward and outward movement. During bars five and six, he gracefully raises it once more; and during bars seven and eight, replaces it firmly on his head. The lady gently draws her free arm inward and upward, and then lowers it downward and outward.

Medium continenzas: These occupy 2 bars each. At the first bar, extend the left foot sideways a few inches, bending both knees outwards. At bar two, join the right foot to the left in the first position, rising on the toes. Sink the heels at the half-bar. Perform the right continenza in similar fashion, moving towards the right.

The arm movements: Move the arms gently in the opposite direction from that in which you step.

The quick reverence (riverenza presta): On the first beat of the bar, place the left toe behind the right heel, bending both knees outwards. At the half-bar, rise again on the toes, straightening both knees. Make the right quick reverence in similar fashion, using the right foot in place of the left.

The zoppetto: To make a left zoppetto, hop on the right foot, raising the left foot forward (or occasionally backward). At the half-bar (third beat), lower the left foot to the ground. In an ornate variation, the zoppetto may be made in double-quick time. This occurs in the man's variation in figure XI, wherein the hop and lifting of the other foot are made in 1 beat, and the lowering of the raised foot on the next beat, thus occupying only the half-bar. This is a *zoppetto presto*. The right zoppetto is made hopping on the left foot and raising the right foot forward.

The galliard step: In this dance, the galliard step (*passo largo in gagliarda*) follows after the zoppetto as used in the concluding section of all the figures except the final one. When following the right zoppetto with a left galliard step, proceed as follows: Having lowered the right toe at the half-bar of bar fourteen, bend the knees outwards and, in anticipation of the first beat of the following bar, advance the left foot and then draw it backward with a wide semicircular movement, round behind the right foot (the left toe just touching the ground as it moves with no weight on it). It arrives behind the right heel, in the fifth position right, on the first beat of bar fifteen. At that instant, rise on the toes of both feet, with straightened knees. At the half-bar, bend the knees outward slightly in preparation for the right cadenza which follows at the sixteenth bar, from which the dancer lands with joined feet in the first position.

The cadenza: The name cadenza, as used in dancing terms, signifies a pause, or full stop after a series of steps. To make a left cadenza, scoop the left foot forward, a little in advance of the beat, and, springing into the air (with both feet off the ground), draw it rapidly back behind the right foot, landing precisely on the beat, in either the third or fourth position. To make a right cadenza, scoop the right foot forward and proceed in the same manner, landing on the beat with the right foot behind the left. Where it happens that the foot governing the cadenza which starts the closing formula is already raised forward, lower it on the final beat of the preceding bar, bending the knees outward to obtain impetus.

The dotted single (puntata grave): This is a single of uneven proportions. To make a left dotted single, diagonally leftwards, tread lightly on the ball of the foot and still keep the weight on the right foot. At the half-bar (third beat), transfer the weight to the left foot, bending both knees and swaying the left hip outwards. On the fourth beat, join the right foot to the left simultaneously rising on the toes of both feet and sinking the heels at the close of the bar.

The slow step (passo grave): This occupies 1 bar and, although in the opening formula it is accompanied by a quick half-reverence (l.), such is merely an ornament superimposed on the right step, which step nevertheless holds throughout the bar. At the first beat of the bar, step forward on the flat of the right foot, and at the half-bar, bend the knee in agreement with the left half-reverence. On the four beat, rise on the toes, with well-straightened knees.

Half-reverence (mezza riverenza presta): The right slow step having been made on the first beat of bar three of the opening formula, proceed as follows: On the second beat, advance the left foot slightly and quickly withdraw it behind the right heel. On the third beat, bend both knees outward; and on the fourth beat, rise on the toes of both feet. Throughout the second half of bar three, the right foot remains in place with the weight resting evenly on both feet. In those figures where the dancers begin with the right foot by way of contrast (consequently making the slow step with the left foot), the half-reverence is made in the same manner, but with the right foot.

The underfoot step (sotto piede): To perform a right underfoot step, spring towards the right on to the right foot, simultaneously raising the left foot behind. On the second beat of the bar, insert the left foot beneath the right heel, chasing the right foot forward, raised several inches from the ground. Each underfoot step occupies half a bar. Make the left underfoot step in similar fashion, springing towards the left.

The hopped flourish: In figure II the series of 8 flourishes employed in the advancing passeggio begins with a right flourish. To make a right hopped flourish, on the first beat, raise the right foot forward a few inches from the ground, simultaneously hopping on the left. At the second beat, draw the right foot back, placing it behind the left heel. At the third beat, slipping it beneath the left foot, chase the left foot forward, raising it a few inches from the ground. Hold this position during the fourth beat, in readiness to make the left flourish in the succeeding bar. If the dancer wishes to increase the rate of advance, a little more ground can be gained with each successive hop.

The balzetti: These are little sideways hops made with feet joined in the first position.

The costatetti: Standing with feet joined in the first position, raise the left foot sideways a short distance (Caroso says 'half a step') from the right. This movement is done in anticipation of the first beat. On the first beat, slip the left foot into the place of the right, tapping the left heel against the right heel. On the second beat, hop on the left foot, raising the right foot sideways a short distance. This constitutes one left costatetto. Make the right costatetto to follow in similar fashion, thus completing the pair of costatetti.

The recacciate: To make a left recacciata, on the first beat, kick the left foot backwards (raised a few inches from the ground), simultaneously hopping on the right. On the second beat, tap the left toe on the ground behind the right heel. On the third beat, insert the left foot beneath the right, chasing the right foot forward, raised two inches from the ground. Hold this position during the fourth beat, resting on the flat of the left foot. To start the right recacciata, kick the right foot backward, while hopping on the left foot, and proceed as described above, using opposite feet. It should be remembered that in figure IV, wherein we meet with the costatetti and the recacciate, the lady is using the opposite foot from that of her partner.

The groppo: This is a group of steps occupying 2 bars and consisting of 3 leaps from side to side, simultaneously kicking the other foot backwards. When making a right groppo, first leap to the right, kicking back with the left foot. At the half-bar (third beat), leap to the left, kicking back with the right foot. On the first beat of bar two, leap once more to the right, kicking back with the left foot; and, on the second beat, insert the left foot beneath the right heel, chasing the right foot forward. At the half-bar, lower the right foot beside the left, in the first position. Make the left groppo in similar fashion, leaping left, right, left, and chasing the left foot forward with the right.

The feigned sequence (seguito finto): This step occurs in the intermediate section of figure XIII (man's variation). Having completed the right backward zoppetto in bar five, the dancer (standing with the right toe lowered beside his left heel, and with his right profile turned to partner) remains on the toes during the fourth beat, ready to perform the left feigned sequence which occupies bar six. On the first beat of the bar, drawing the left toe backwards with an outward-curved movement, he places it behind the right heel, remaining on the toes, with straightened knees. On the second beat, he draws back the right foot with the same outward curve and places it beside the left, in the first position. On the third beat he steps forward on the flat of the left foot, placing it in front of the right, in the fifth position left, and lowers the right heel. On the fourth beat, rising on the toes, he makes a half-turn right, so as to present left profile to partner. He will now be standing in the fifth position right. During bar seven, he performs the right feigned sequence in similar fashion, starting with the right foot. On the fourth beat he rises on the toes, but continues to face towards the right, while making the left backward zoppetto which occupies the eighth bar, during which he remains on the toes.

The quick steps (passi presti): These follow after the foregoing left zoppetto, and are made lightly, the dancer almost springing from foot to foot. The first 2 steps are made on the toes, and the third on the ball of the foot (r.l.r.). They occupy 1 beat each. On the fourth beat, the dancer rises on the toes and makes a half-turn left, on the right toe, in preparation for the second set of 3 quick steps (l.r.l.). At the close of these the dancer makes a quarter-turn right on the left toe, so as to face forward, raising the right foot sideways, in readiness for the pair of sideways flourishes which follow.

The sideways flourishes (fioretti fiancheggiati a piedi pari): These flourishes occupy 1 bar each. The dancer stands on the left foot, with the right pointing sideways a few inches from the ground. On the first beat, he lowers the right foot beside the left, tapping the ground with the toe and, simultaneously, lifting the left an inch or so. On the second beat, he taps the ground with the left toe, beside the right, which he lifts slightly. On the third beat, he taps the ground with the ball of the right foot, giving a sharper accent than before, at the same time pointing the left foot sideways, raised a few inches from the ground. He holds this position during the fourth beat. This completes the right sideways flourish, which is followed by the left flourish, performed in similar fashion. All the movements should be small and neat.

The gliding sequences (seguiti scorsi): These occupy the whole of the lady's variation in figure XIII, and are divided into 2 circles (l.r.). They consist of a series of tiny half-steps, smoothly made on the toes. When circling towards the left, the dancer should keep the left foot foremost, bringing up the right only as far as the left heel; whereas, when moving towards the right, she should keep the right foot foremost. The head should be turned in the direction in which she is moving and the arms held in the opposite direction, gracefully curved. This passeggio is very effective.

The slow steps (passi gravi): These occur in the final figure and occupy 1 bar each. The dancer steps forward on the flat of the foot, rising at the half-bar on to the ball of the foot (l.r.l.). At the fourth bar he pauses, pointing the right foot forward. After the 3 retreating steps (r.l.r.), he again pauses, pointing the left forward.

The quick cabrioles (capriole preste): These conclude the man's part in figure VIII, and occupy half a bar each. The feet pass each other three times with each jump. If preferred, the usual cadenza may be made in place of the 2 cabrioles.

PAVANIGLIA

HACHAS

(*A Torch Dance*)

In an account of the festivities held in celebration of the marriage of Lucrezia Borgia to Alfonso d'Este, written by Isabella d'Este to her husband Francesco, Marquess of Mantua (3 February 1502), there occurs a reference to a torch dance, as follows: 'About six o'clock the first play began ... the Moresche dances between the acts were very well danced, and with great spirit ... The last was danced by Moors with lighted torches in their hands, and was a fine sight.'[1] Cesare Negri provides us with two examples of this type of dance, as performed at the Court of Milan during the wedding festivities of the Infanta Isabella of Spain and her consort, the Archduke Alberto of Austria. I here present the second of these, and have chosen (in preference to the rather humdrum tune given by Negri) a fine old Spanish one whose theme admits of much repetition without ever tiring the listener.

Negri describes an elaborate opening ceremony. First there enter four musicians, accom-

[1] *Isabella d'Este*, Julia Cartright.

panied by four Swiss Guards 'in livery'. These are followed by six pages carrying lighted torches. Four of these enter in couples and are followed by the remaining two, acting as escort to the god of Love, who walks between them and later on recites some verses in praise of the august bridal pair. This diversion is succeeded by the appearance on the scene of six noble cavaliers dressed in Hungarian costume, who also carry lighted torches. They walk in couples, those to the left holding the torch in their left hand, and their partners holding theirs in the right hand, whilst they perform an ornate *Intrada* which closes with their formation in a crescent-shaped line. Advancing their torches in salute, they execute a profound reverence. At this point they halt while the god of Love comes to the front and recites his rather lengthy ode, the text of which is given in Negri's book on an adjoining page. At the conclusion he retires, escorted by the pages, and the main dance begins.

For those who wish to perform the dance independently of this opening ceremony, I would suggest the following arrangement as producing a pleasing and impressive effect.

Entry of six pages

The six pages who act as ushers should enter in procession, two and two, carrying their torches in the outside hand. They enter from the centre of the back stage and, using the formula of 2 broken singles and 1 broken double (repeated), advance towards the front of the stage. This completes the first strain. The leaders then cast off, those on the left veering round in that direction and proceeding towards back stage (with 2 broken singles and 1 broken double, repeated), where they take up their position across the corner on that side. The dancers on the right simultaneously go through the same evolution, veering to the right and taking their stand at the opposite corner. Here they remain, stationary. At the beginning of the second strain, the six cavaliers enter, two by two, from the centre of the back stage, and with the same order of steps, go through a similar evolution on a more restricted scale, making their steps a little smaller so as to finish up in the centre in double file, a few paces in advance of the back stage. The torches must always be held in the outside hand.

Now the cavaliers start their formal *Intrada*: Advancing with 2 broken doubles (l.r.), the right and left dancers of each couple cross each other's path diagonally, each left-hand dancer passing in front of the right. Having accomplished this oblique advance (changing places), the partners turn to face each other and perform 2 side-jumps (*balzetti*) with the feet joined in the first position. This is followed by 4 stationary steps (l.r.l.r.) made by springing on to each toe in turn, in the manner of marking time. This completes the first strain. During the repeat, they continue their advance in the same manner, crossing obliquely into each other's places and then performing the 2 balzetti (l.r.) and 4 stationary steps face to face. During the second strain, they once more go through the same formula. The repeat brings the entry to a close in the following manner: During the first 4 bars they range themselves in a crescent-shaped row, facing the audience. This is accomplished (speaking from the point of view of the dancers) as follows. The leading couple advance obliquely leftwards with 2 broken doubles, while the second couple advance simultaneously to the right with 2 broken doubles, and the third couple, taking rather larger steps, advance in a like manner, directly forward. Having completed this manœuvre during the first 4 bars of the repeat, the dancers advance their torches in salutation to the onlookers, at the same time making a deep reverence of 4 bars' duration. This brings us to the end of the strain and concludes the *Intrada*. The dancers reform in a double row, facing leftwards across the stage, so that their right profile is turned towards the spectators. There should be a slight pause on the final chord while this readjustment takes place. The left-hand man in each couple makes a quarter-turn left on his right toe while his partner, turning on his left toe, wheels round beside him, stepping with the right foot. The dance proper now begins.

FIGURE I

During the first strain, the leading couple cast off to right and left, followed by the others. The steps employed for this evolution are 2 broken singles and 1 broken double, beginning with the left foot, and the same again, beginning with the right foot. During the repeat, the first couple lead up the middle, hand in hand, with 2 broken doubles, while the other two couples follow in their wake, all returning to their original positions. This passage occupies the first half of the repeat. In the second half the partners turn face to face, and perform the 2 balzetti (l.r.) and the 4 springing, stationary steps, as in the *Intrada*. During the first half of the second strain all the partners link right arms (holding their torches in the left hand) and pass into each other's places, turning round leftwards after passing, so as to come face to face again. The steps employed are 2 broken doubles (l.r.). During the second half of the strain, they perform 2 diminished reprises (l.r.). At the repeat of the strain, the two leading dancers turn to face those of their own side and execute a chain figure down the line and up with their respective followers, by means of 8 broken singles, giving alternately the right and left hand, each time shifting the torch to the other hand. The dancers, on reaching the end of the line, execute (before returning) a circle, as though turning with an imaginary person. At the close, when back in their original places, the dancers fill in any remaining bars or beats by circling on their own axis. As there are three dancers in each row, every dancer gives his hand four times.

FIGURE II

The partners turn face to face, and, giving their right hands, cross over into each other's places with 1 broken double (l.). Giving their left hands, they cross back again with another broken double (r.), making a half-turn leftwards at the close. This brings us to the half of the strain. During the second half, each dancer describes a circle leftwards with 2 more broken doubles (l.r.), coming face to face with partner at the close. The repeat is devoted to an ingenious chain figure. The dancer at the head of the right-hand file crosses over diagonally with the dancer at the foot of the left-hand file. In passing, they take right arms or hands and swing round into each other's places. Turning to face the middle man in their respective lines, they start a chain figure, giving the left hand, while simultaneously the two end men at the opposite corners (top left-hand file and lowest right-hand file) cross diagonally into each other's places, also giving the left hand, or arm, as they swing round. They in turn face the middle man and start to pass along the line in a chain figure, giving the right hand, while simultaneously the one who is now left top man crosses diagonally with the lowest right-hand man, also giving the right hand or arm. They continue these evolutions until all have returned to their original places. The two who have started the figure with the diagonal change of place (while the other four dancers are as yet stationary), are in consequence the first to regain their proper places, where they pause while their companions complete the figure. When all are back in position, there should remain 1 bar of music during which all revolve with 1 broken single. The complete figure is performed with 8 broken singles, each interchange of place being achieved with 1 broken single, occupying 1 bar of the music.

During the second strain the pairs of dancers part company. The left-hand leader turns to his left and leads his followers round towards back stage with 2 broken singles (l.r.) and 1 broken double (l.), followed by 2 broken singles (r.l.) and 1 broken double (r.). Simultaneously the right-hand leader will have wheeled round towards his right and led his file round the opposite side of the stage with the same order of steps, so that the two leaders meet in the centre near to the back of the stage. They turn to face the spectators, and their followers line up at either side, the whole row thus forming a concave crescent shape. This completes the second strain. During the repeat the dancers make 2 slow backward reprises, occupying 2 bars each, followed by a Grand Reverence (with torches advanced in salute) occupying the last 4 bars.

Finale

The two leaders, followed by the other dancers and the six pages, advance two by two towards the front of the stage with 2 broken singles (l.r.) and 1 broken double (l.), and the same again, beginning with the right foot. They now separate, and, with the same order of steps throughout, they veer round to left and right respectively towards back stage, until they meet in the middle and lead out through the central exit.

HOW TO PERFORM THE SINGLES AND DOUBLES

For a left broken single: On the first beat of the bar, step forward on the flat of the left foot. On the second beat, rising on the toes, place the right toe behind the left heel. On the third beat, advance the left foot, on the flat of the foot, and hold it thus during the fourth beat. Perform the right single in similar fashion.

Four Dances of Spanish Origin: Spagnoletto, Villanos, Pavaniglia, Hachas

For a left broken double: This occupies 2 bars. On the first beat of bar one, step forward on the left toe, and on the third beat, step forward on the right toe. On the first beat of bar two, step forward on the flat of the left foot, and on the second beat, rising on the toes, place the right toe behind the left heel. On the third beat, advance the left foot again, on the flat of the foot, and hold it thus during the fourth beat.

The balzetti: These are little sideways hops, made with feet joined in the first position.

The reverence: During the first bar, stand with the left foot advanced. At bar two, draw it back behind the right, inclining the head and body. At bar three, join it to the right (first position), rising on the toes and straightening the head and body. At bar four, sink the heels.

HACHAS (A TORCH DANCE)

CHAPTER VII

Two Italian Dances: Passomezzo, La Nizzarda

PASSOMEZZO

THE dance named *Passomezzo* is the Italian version of an ornate pavan, and has a strong affinity with the 'Spanish Pavan' as described in the last chapter. The Italian name has been subjected to various corruptions, such as Arbeau's *passemeze*, Caroso's *passo e mezo* and Sir Toby Belch's 'passy measure pavin'. The original name was *passomezzo*, meaning the 'half-step', since its movements and tempo were quickened in that proportion, as contrasted with the solemn processional pavan. In a lute manuscript, dating *c.* 1555 and bearing on its outside page the arms of the Medici, which Arnold Dolmetsch acquired in Florence, there occurs a very fine example of a *passomezzo* tune, entitled *Passomezzo del Giorgio*. It is this tune that I propose to use in conjunction with Caroso's first version of this interesting dance which he qualifies as *d'incerto*, meaning of unknown date and origin. The dance contains fourteen figures, from which I select seven typical examples, and is described as for a single couple.

FIGURE I

Opening salutations and passeggio

The music consists of 2 strains of 16 bars each. The partners stand face to face, without holding hands, and perform the Grand Reverence, occupying 8 bars. This is followed by 2 continenzas of 4 bars each, thus bringing us to the end of the first strain.

During the second strain, they perform their passeggio, wheeling round clockwise for the first half of the strain, with the man holding the lady's right hand in his own right (lifted shoulder high). During the second half, they reverse their motion, with the man holding the lady's left hand in his own left, and both wheeling round anti-clockwise. The steps employed are as follows: They begin with 2 slow steps (l.r.) occupying bars one and two. In bars three and four they make an ordinary sequence (*seguito ordinario*) consisting of 2 quick steps (l.r.) and 1 slow one (l.). During bars five and six, they make 1 slow step (r.) followed by 2 quick ones (l.r.). Bar seven is occupied by a left side-leap (*trabuchetto*) face to face, with the right foot lowered beside the left at the half-bar; and at bar eight, they make a little jump with joined feet (*balzetto*) towards the right. Taking left hands (lifted shoulder high) they then wheel round anti-clockwise, with the same series of steps as in the first half, but beginning with the right foot. At the close, they release hands.

FIGURE II

Man's variation and lady's passeggio

The stationary variation in this type of dance is termed a *mutanza*, and is of a florid character. The man stands opposite his partner and performs his variation, while she, pacing alternately to left and right, performs the same series of steps as used in the passeggio of figure I (second strain). For the first four bars she turns leftwards. In bars five and six she turns to the right; and during bars seven and eight she faces partner. In the second half, she turns first right, then left, facing partner for the last 2 bars.

The man, during bar one, makes a quick reverence (*riverenza presta*) with the left foot behind the right, in the fifth position. In bar two, he makes a left zoppetto, hopping on the right foot, with left raised forward and lowered at the half-bar. During bar three, he makes a right galliard step (*passo fermato in gagliarda*), and in bar four, a right cadenza. Bars five and six are occupied by a series of leaping steps, termed a *groppo*, and bar seven by a left side-leap and a right underfoot step (both *presto*). In bar eight, he makes a quick reverence (r.). During bars nine and ten he performs a series of toe-and-heel steps (*punto e calcagno*), first with the left foot and then with the right. In the eleventh bar, he makes a right side-leap and an underfoot chasing-step to the left; and in bar twelve, he performs a quick reverence (l.). The last 4 bars are occupied by a left cadenza, left zoppetto, right galliard step and right cadenza. This completes the first strain of the melody.

During the lady's simultaneous passeggio, she keeps her head turned towards the partner, as she paces to left and right, and in making the side-leap and balzetto, she turns to face him directly.

FIGURE III

Lady's variation and man's passeggio

This figure occupies the second strain of the melody and consists of the lady's ornate variation and the man's simultaneous passeggio in which he paces to and fro, to left and right, with head turned towards partner.

The lady starts her variation with 2 broken-sequences (*seguiti spezzati*) occupying 4 bars in all (l.r.) followed by 3 slow side-leaps (*trabuchetti gravi*), beginning with the left foot, and terminating with joined feet. These occupy another 4 bars and bring us to the half of the strain. The same series of steps is repeated, beginning with the right foot, thus bringing us to the end of the second strain.

The man's simultaneous passeggio runs as follows: First he makes 2 slow steps (l.r.) and 1 left broken double (*seguito semidoppio*), turning leftwards. This occupies 4 bars. Then, turning to the right, he repeats the same steps, beginning with the right foot. This brings us to the half of the strain. Turning once more leftwards, on the right toe, he makes 2 quick steps (l.r.), occupying 1 bar together, and 3 hopped flourishes of one bar each (l.r.l.). He now makes a quarter-turn right, so as to face partner, and occupies the remaining 4 bars with a right cadenza, a left galliard step, a right galliard step and a right cadenza, finishing with the feet joined in the first position (after the manner of *Pavaniglia*, as Caroso remarks).

FIGURE IV

Intermediate passeggio together

The man takes his partner's right hand in his own (lifted shoulder high), and they wheel round clockwise. In the first 2 bars, they make 2 hopped steps (l.r.), followed in the third and fourth bars by 2 hopped flourishes. This series of steps is repeated in the next 4 bars and again in the following 4, thus bringing us to the end of the twelfth bar. They release hands and, during bars thirteen and fourteen, turning face to face, they perform a left side-leap and a right underfoot step, lowering the right foot at the fifteenth bar. At bar sixteen they make a right balzetto with joined feet, bending the knees slightly outwards, and rising again. At the close of the bar they make a rapid quarter-turn right on the left toe. During the second strain, the man takes the lady's left hand in his own left, and they wheel round anti-clockwise, performing the same series of steps as used in the first strain, but beginning with the right foot and sinking the heels at the close of the sixteenth bar.

FIGURE V

Man's variation and lady's passeggio

The man remains turned towards his partner, and, in bars one and two, makes a left dotted single (*puntata grave*), advancing diagonally leftwards, and in bars three and four, 2 stationary hopped flourishes (r.l.). In bars five and six he makes a sideways dotted single (r.), retreating; and in bars seven and eight, two stationary hopped flourishes (l.r.), facing forward. This brings us to the half of the strain. In bars nine and ten, he revolves to the left by means of 2 slow steps (*passi gravi*), which occupy 1 bar each. To effect this revolution, he first places the left toe behind the right heel, raising the right foot forward a few inches, and spins round a half-turn. Then, bringing the right toe down in front of the left, and raising the left foot backwards, he spins round another half-turn leftwards, so as to face forward at the close. This brings us to the end of bar ten. In the eleventh and twelfth bars, he makes 2 hopped flourishes (l.r.), advancing; and during the thirteenth and fourteenth bars, he performs a left side-leap, followed by a right side-leap. On the first beat of bar fifteen, he makes a left underfoot step (*presto*), and at bar sixteen, a right balzetto, sinking the heels at the close of the bar.

Throughout this variation, the lady performs her passeggio as in figures I and II, pacing to left and right.

FIGURE VI

Lady's variation and man's passeggio

The lady's variation starts with 2 slow reprises (*riprese grave*) in retreat (l.r.). These occupy 1 bar each. In bars three and four, she makes 2 side-leaps (l.r.). These are followed by 2 broken-sequences (*seguiti spezzati*), advancing, occupying 2 bars each. This brings us to the half of the strain. During bars nine and ten, she revolves leftwards with 2 slow steps (l.r.) in the same manner as that described in the man's preceding variation. In bars eleven and twelve, she makes a broken-sequence (*seguito spezzato*), advancing (l.). During the last 4 bars, she makes 3 side-leaps (r.l.r.), lowering the left foot beside the right at the sixteenth bar.

Man's passeggio

The man's simultaneous passeggio is performed as in figure III.

Two Italian Dances: Passomezzo, La Nizzarda

FIGURE VII

Passeggio for both dancers wheeling round

As there are some important divergences in the character of the steps employed by the two dancers, I will describe them individually. In this passage they rotate clockwise throughout.

The man takes the lady's right hand in his own, and, in bars one and two, makes 2 hopped flourishes (l.r.), wheeling round. He then releases her hand and, turning to face her, makes a high cut caper (*capriola spezzata in aria*) in the space of bars three and four. In bars five and six, taking her right hand again, he makes 2 more hopped flourishes (l.r.), wheeling round. In bars seven and eight, releasing her hand, he faces her with another cut caper. In bars nine and ten, taking her right hand again, he makes 2 more hopped flourishes (l.r.), wheeling round. During bar eleven, he releases her hand and, turning to face her, makes a rapid left side-leap (*trabuchetto presto*) and a double quick underfoot step to the right. He keeps the right foot raised at the end of the bar and, during bar twelve, makes a right hopped flourish, facing toward partner. In bar thirteen, he makes a left side-leap, and at bar fourteen, lowers the raised right foot beside the left, rising on the toes. At bar fifteen, bending the knees to gain impetus, he springs high into the air, passing the feet five times and alighting at bar sixteen with grace and dexterity. This is a *capriola in quinta*.

Lady's passeggio

The lady's passeggio runs as follows: Giving her right hand to her partner, held shoulder high, she makes 2 hopped flourishes (l.r.), wheeling round. This occupies the first 2 bars. Releasing hands, she makes during the third and fourth bars, 2 side-leaps (l.r.), facing her partner. During the following 4 bars, she repeats the same series of steps. This brings us to the half of the strain. In bars nine and ten, she makes 2 hopped flourishes (l.r.), facing partner; and in bars eleven and twelve, she makes 2 more hopped flourishes (l.r.), revolving clockwise on her own axis. At bar thirteen, facing partner, she makes a left side-leap, and at bar fourteen, lowers the raised right foot beside the left, rising on the toes. At bar fifteen, she bends and rises again; and at bar sixteen, she makes a right balzetto. This brings us to the end of the first strain.

Closing salutations

Standing face to face, without holding hands, the partners bring the dance to a close with 2 slow continenzas (l.r.), occupying 8 bars in all, followed by the Grand Reverence, which occupies the remaining 8 bars of the second strain.

Two Italian Dances: Passomezzo, La Nizzarda

The order of the steps

FIGURE I

Grand Reverence	8 bars
2 continenzas l.r.	8 bars
	16 bars

Passeggio together
(Take right hands)

2 slow steps l.r. (clockwise)	2 bars
1 ordinary sequence l.r.l.	2 bars
1 slow step r.	1 bar
2 quick steps l.r. (release hands)	1 bar
1 side-leap l. (facing partner)	1 bar
1 balzetto r. (joined feet)	1 bar
	8 bars

(Take left hands)

2 slow steps r.l. (anti-clockwise)	2 bars
1 ordinary sequence r.l.r.	2 bars
1 slow step l.	1 bar
2 quick steps r.l.	1 bar
1 side-leap r.; join feet	1 bar
1 balzetto l.	1 bar
	8 bars

FIGURE II

Man's stationary variation

Quick reverence l.	1 bar
Zoppetto (left foot raised)	1 bar
Right galliard step	1 bar
Right cadenza	1 bar
Groppo l.r.l.r.	2 bars
Left side-leap and right underfoot step	1 bar
Quick reverence r.	1 bar
	8 bars

Toe-and-heel steps l.r.	2 bars
Right side-leap and left underfoot step	1 bar
Quick reverence l.	1 bar
Left cadenza	1 bar
Zoppetto (left foot raised)	1 bar
Right galliard step	1 bar
Right cadenza (landing in first position)	1 bar
	8 bars

Lady's simultaneous passeggio

2 slow steps l.r. (turning left)	2 bars
1 ordinary sequence l.r.l.	2 bars
1 slow step r. (turning right)	1 bar
2 quick steps l.r.	1 bar
Left side-leap; join right foot to left	1 bar
1 balzetto r.	1 bar
	8 bars

Repeat same, beginning with right foot, and turning to right and left	8 bars

FIGURE III

Lady's variation

2 broken-sequences l.r. (sideways)	4 bars
3 side-leaps l.r.l.	3 bars
Join right foot to left (first position)	1 bar
2 broken-sequences r.l. (sideways)	4 bars
3 side-leaps r.l.r.	3 bars
Join left foot to right (first position)	1 bar
	16 bars

Man's simultaneous passeggio

2 slow steps l.r. (turning left)	2 bars
1 left broken double	2 bars
2 slow steps r.l. (turning right)	2 bars
1 right broken double	2 bars
2 quick steps l.r. (turning left)	1 bar
3 hopped flourishes l.r.l.	3 bars

(*Turn to face partner*)

Right cadenza	1 bar
Left galliard step	1 bar
Right galliard step	1 bar
Right cadenza (landing in first position)	1 bar
	16 bars

FIGURE IV

Intermediate passeggio both together
(*Take right hands*)

{ 2 hopped steps l.r. (clockwise)	2 bars
{ 2 hopped flourishes l.r.	2 bars
Repeat same series of steps l.r.	4 bars
Repeat same series of steps l.r.	4 bars

(*Release hands*)

Left side-leap (face to face)	1 bar
Right underfoot step	1 bar
Join right foot to left	1 bar
1 balzetto r.	1 bar
	16 bars

(*Take left hands*)

Repeat same passeggio (wheeling anti-clockwise), beginning with right foot	16 bars

FIGURE V

Man's variation

(*Facing partner*)

1 slow dotted single l. (advancing)	2 bars
2 hopped flourishes r.l.	2 bars
1 slow dotted single r. (retreating)	2 bars
2 hopped flourishes l.r.	2 bars
2 slow steps l.r. (revolving left)	2 bars
2 hopped flourishes l.r.	2 bars
Left side-leap	1 bar
Right side-leap	1 bar
1 underfoot step (presto); join feet	1 bar
1 balzetto r.	1 bar
	16 bars

Lady's simultaneous passeggio

This is performed as in figure II 16 bars

FIGURE VI

Lady's variation

(*Facing partner*)

2 slow reprises (retreating)	2 bars
2 side-leaps l.r.	2 bars
2 broken-sequences l.r. (advancing zigzag)	4 bars
2 slow steps revolving left	2 bars
1 broken-sequence l. (advancing)	2 bars
3 side-leaps r.l.r.	3 bars
Join left foot to right, and sink heels	1 bar
	16 bars

Man's simultaneous passeggio

This is performed as in figure III 16 bars

FIGURE VII

Finale

Passeggio together, wheeling clockwise

Man's Steps	Lady's Steps	
(Take right hands)		
2 hopped flourishes l.r.	2 hopped flourishes l.r.	2 bars
(Release hands)		
Cut caper, face to face	2 side-leaps l.r.	2 bars
(Take right hands)		
2 hopped flourishes l.r.	2 hopped flourishes l.r.	2 bars
(Release hands)		
Cut caper, face to face	2 side-leaps l.r.	2 bars
(Take right hands)		
2 hopped flourishes l.r.	2 hopped flourishes l.r.	2 bars
(Face partner; release hands)		
Side-leap l.; underfoot r.; hopped flourish r.	2 hopped flourishes l.r., revolving	2 bars
Side-leap l.; join right foot to left	Side-leap l.; join right foot to left	2 bars
Capriola in quinto	Bend, rise, balzetto r.	2 bars
		16 bars

If the man should prefer to perform the same steps as those of his partner, throughout this finale, he may quite well do so. In that case there is no need to release hands until bar eleven, when the hopped flourishes are made revolving independently. To my thinking, this arrangement produces a more pleasing ensemble than that in which the continuity is interrupted by the man's cut capers, however agile.

Closing salutations

2 continenzas l.r.	8 bars
Grand Reverence	8 bars
	16 bars

Two Italian Dances: Passomezzo, La Nizzarda

HOW TO PERFORM THE STEPS

The Grand Reverence: In this dance, wherein the bars are halved in length as compared with the *Pavan*, the Grand Reverence occupies 8 bars, and is performed exactly as described in the directions for *Pavaniglia*, including those for the arm movements and the removal of the man's hat (Chapter VI).

The two continenzas: In the *Passomezzo* here described, the continenzas occupy 4 bars each. To make the left continenza, step sideways on the flat of the left foot, bending the knee a little. At bar two, rise on the toes. At bar three, join the right foot to the left in the first position and, at bar four, sink the left heel. The hip should be advanced slightly in the direction in which the dancer is moving. Perform the right continenza in similar fashion.

The slow steps (passi gravi): These occupy 1 bar each. On the first beat, step forward on the flat of the foot, and at the half bar, rise on the toes. The dancer sways gently in the direction of the stepping foot.

The quick steps (passi presti): These are made lightly on the ball of the foot, with straightened knees, and occupy half a bar each.

The ordinary sequence (seguito ordinario): This occupies 2 bars. To make a left sequence, step forward lightly on the ball of the left foot, on the first beat of bar one, and at the half-bar, step forward on the ball of the right foot. At bar two, step forward on the flat of the left foot, and at the half-bar, rise on the toes. Make the right sequence in similar fashion, beginning with the right foot.

The side-leaps (trabuchetti): When leaping to the left, land on the left toe, raising the right foot forward in front of the left with the toe well pointed and the knees straightened. Make the right side-leap in similar fashion, landing on the right toe, with the left foot raised in front.

The balzetti: These are little sideways hops with the feet joined in the first position. On alighting, the dancer should bend the knees slightly and immediately rise again, with the knees well straightened.

Quick reverence: This action is a quick bend and rise, with the feet in the fifth position. When the left foot is at the back, this constitutes a *left* quick reverence, and the reverse position constitutes a *right* quick reverence.

The zoppetto: To make a left zoppetto, hop on the right foot, raising the left foot forward (or *occasionally* backward). At the half-bar, lower the left foot to the ground. The right zoppetto is made hopping on the left foot and raising the right. The name zoppetto means a limping hop.

The cadenza: The name cadenza, in dancing terms, means a pause, or full stop, closing a series of steps. To make a left cadenza, scoop the left foot forward, a little in advance of the beat, simultaneously springing into the air. Then drawing it back, the dancer lands on the beat in the third or fourth position. When it occurs at the close of a figure, the dancer sometimes lands with feet joined in the first position. This happens both in *Pavaniglia* and in the *Passomezzo*.

The groppo: This is a group of steps occupying 2 bars, and consisting of 3 leaps from side to side, with alternating feet, simultaneously kicking the other foot backwards. When making a left groppo, leap first to the left, kicking the right foot backwards. At the half-bar, leap to the right, kicking back with the left foot. On the first beat of bar two, leap once more to the left, kicking back with the right foot, and immediately insert the right foot beneath the left heel, chasing the left foot forward. At the half-bar, lower the left foot beside the right in the first position.

The galliard step (passo largo in gagliarda): This step occupies 1 bar and is done smoothly. To make the left galliard step, stand on the flat of the right foot, with slightly bent knee, and, advancing the left foot, draw it back again, trailed along the ground with a wide semi-circular movement. As you join it to the right foot, rise on the toes, with straightened knees.

The toe-and-heel step (punto e calcagno): These are made hopping on the one foot and tapping the ground with the other, alternately on the toe and the heel. For the left toe and heel, hop on the right foot and tap with the left, beside the right, a few inches distant from it.

The broken-sequences (seguiti spezzati): These take 2 bars, and in the *Passomezzo*, should be made with a bending and rising movement, and a hop at the end, in saltarello style, swaying in the direction of the stepping foot. To make a left broken-sequence, step forward on the flat of the left foot, bending the knee slightly and swaying towards the left. At the half-bar, rise on the toes and slide the right toe up level with the left heel. On the first beat of bar two, advance the left foot once more, on the flat of the foot, and at the half-bar, rising on the toes, hop on the left foot, raising the right foot forward a few inches. For a left sequence it produces a good effect to veer slightly towards the left, and for a right sequence towards the right.

Hopped flourishes (fioretti spezzati): These occupy 1 bar each. To make a left hopped flourish, raise the left foot forward a few inches; and on the first beat, hop on the right foot. At the second beat, draw the left foot back level with the right heel, tapping the ground with the tip of the toe. At the half-bar (third beat), insert the left foot beneath the right heel, chasing the right foot forward. If it is desired to advance by means of the flourishes, this is effected by the hops, which may be forward, backward or stationary. Make the right flourish in similar fashion raising the right foot forward. The music of the *Passomezzo* (in common with that of the Spanish *Pavan*) is in duple time. For the description of the steps, however, which are mostly ornamented, I have to subdivide these beats into four, to give to the movements their exact proportions.

The underfoot steps (sotto piedi): To perform a left underfoot step, spring sideways on to the left foot, simultaneously raising the right foot behind. On the second beat, insert the right toe beneath the left heel, chasing the left foot forward. Perform the right underfoot step in similar fashion, towards the right.

NIZZARDA

PASSOMEZZO

Two Italian Dances: Passomezzo, La Nizzarda

The dotted singles: These occupy 2 bars each. On the first beat of bar one, step forward (or backward) obliquely on the ball of the foot, resting the weight on the other foot. On the first beat of bar two, transfer the weight on to the foot which has made the step, bending the knees slightly. At the half-bar, join up the other foot in the first position, rising on the toes with straightened knees. Draw the arms in the opposite direction.

The cut caper (capriola spezzata in aria): This occupies 2 bars.

For a left cut caper, stand with the weight resting on the right foot, and with the left foot raised forward. During the first half of bar one, make 3 springing stationary steps, with a pause on the third (l.r.l.), drawing back the springing foot and raising the other forward, as though marking time. During the second half of bar one, make 3 more (l.r.l.). On the first beat of bar two, lower the left foot behind the right (third position right) and spring high into the air, passing the feet three times, and landing lightly on the toes, in the third position left. There should be a slight bend and rise as the dancer alights. Caroso specifies a double cut caper; but in this, he is referring to the two sets of springing steps, which, he says, are brought to a perfect close by a *capriola in terzo*.

Capriola in quinto: This is a simple cabriole in which the feet pass each other five times. The bend and upward spring should be made during bar one, so that the dancer can alight on the first beat of bar two, bending and rising during the first half, and sinking the heels at the third beat.

PASSOMEZZO DEL GIORGIO

125

LA NIZZARDA

The name of *La Nizzarda* means 'the dance of Nice', the preservation of which gay and cheerful dance, we owe to Cesare Negri. His description makes it clear that *La Nizzarda* was a near relative of *La Volta*, since it resembles one of the versions of this dance alluded to by Thoinot Arbeau, in his treatise *Orchésographie*. Each of these two writers describes the particular version which he considers preferable, and so, having already presented Arbeau's choice (under the title *La Volta*) in my previous book,[1] I will now give you the form approved by Negri, and entitled by him '*La Nizzarda*'.

The dance opens with a passeggio, which the couples dance hand in hand (the lady on her partner's right), circling the room. This first strain consists of 12 bars of music in triple time, and comprising four series of steps, each set occupying 3 bars, and beginning alternately with the left and right foot. The formula goes as follows: On the first beat of bar one, step forward on the left toe, and on the third beat, step forward on the right toe. On the first beat of bar two, make a left zoppetto (hopping on the right foot). On the second beat, lower the left foot; and on the third beat, bend both knees and spring into the air, landing on the first beat of bar three. In making this cadenza, the right foot (which was behind the left) is scooped forward and drawn back again, so that the dancer alights in the third position left. During the ensuing three bars, make a similar series of steps, beginning with the right foot. Follow on with another set, beginning with the left foot, and yet another, with the right foot. During the second strain (consisting of 8 bars), the partners turn face to face, the man holding his partner by both hands. During the first bar they make 3 underfoot steps (*sotto piedi*) sideways, the man leaping on to his left foot, and the lady on to her right, after which they make a straight jump (still hand in hand), landing

[1] *Dances of England and France* (Routledge and Kegan Paul).

126

on the second beat of bar four. In making this jump, they draw their hands inward and upward, and as they alight, they draw them downward and outward. This imparts an appearance of buoyancy which is very pleasing. During the next 2 bars, the same set of steps is repeated in the opposite direction, the man leaping on to his right foot, and the lady on to her left. This brings us to the middle of the strain. The second half is an exact repetition of the first half. I would here mention that the unaccented third beat which introduces each strain, is ignored, the first beat of the ensuing bar being taken as the starting-point. At the close of the dance, the final pause compensates for the last clipped bar. The third strain, which occupies 8 bars, contains the turning movement characteristic of *La Volta*; but it is performed in a different manner. The partners remain face to face, the lady placing her hands on the man's shoulders and he putting his hands on either side of her waist. The man's procedure differs from that of his partner; so I will describe each separately. The series of movements employed occupies 2 bars and is repeated throughout the strain. On the first beat of bar one, the man makes a *left* chasing-step (*recacciata*) occupying 2 beats. On the third beat, he moves the right foot (which will have been projected forward) round behind the left, in the fifth position, and bends both knees. On the first beat of bar two (rising on the toes, and grasping his partner firmly on either side of her waist), he makes a quarter-turn right, tossing her upward as high as is comfortably possible, so that she may alight on the second beat of the bar, when he bends both knees slightly. On the third beat, he rises on the toes. The lady's series of movements is as follows: On the first beat of bar one, she makes a right chasing-step (*recacciata*) occupying 2 beats. On the third beat, she moves the left foot (which will have been projected forward), round beside the right, but distant from it about four inches (second position), bending the knees slightly. On the first beat of bar two, she makes an upward spring, propelled by her partner and leaning her hands on his shoulders. On the second beat, she alights with feet joined in the first position, bending the knees, and on the third beat she rises on the toes. Please note that the knees must always be bent outwards. The above series of steps is performed four times in all, thus bringing us to the end of the strain. The second and third strains are repeated and concluded by a final repeat of the second strain. This closes the dance; but, if it should be performed on a stage, and the dancers should wish to dance off, they can do this to the steps and music of the opening passeggio.

Two Italian Dances: Passomezzo, La Nizzarda

The order of the steps

Passeggio (hand in hand)

2 small steps l.r.	1 bar
Left zoppetto	1 bar
Right cadenza	1 bar
2 small steps r.l.	1 bar
Right zoppetto	1 bar
Left cadenza	1 bar
	6 bars
Repeat this series of steps during the second half of the strain	6 bars
	12 bars

SECOND STRAIN

(Face to face)

3 underfoot steps (man left, lady right)	1 bar
Join feet; bend; straight jump	1 bar
3 underfoot steps (man right, lady left)	1 bar
Join feet; bend; straight jump	1 bar
	4 bars
Repeat same series of steps	4 bars
Total	8 bars

THIRD STRAIN

(*Face to face*)

Man's steps

1 left recacciata ⎫	
Place right toe behind left heel ⎭	1 bar
Make quarter-turn right and project	
partner upwards	1 bar
(Repeat these movements three	
more times)	6 bars
	8 bars

Lady's steps

One right recacciata ⎫	
Left sideways step ⎭	1 bar
High jump	1 bar
(Repeat these movements	
three more times)	6 bars
	8 bars

HOW TO PERFORM THE STEPS

The small steps: Make these springily, on the ball of the foot.

The zoppetto: To make a left zoppetto, hop on the right foot, raising the left foot forward. At the half-bar, lower it beside the right. Perform the right zoppetto in similar fashion, hopping on the left foot and raising the right foot forward.

The cadenza: To make a left cadenza, scoop the left foot forward, a little in advance of the beat, simultaneously springing into the air. Then drawing it back again, land on the beat in the third or fourth position.

The underfoot steps (sotto piedi): To perform a left underfoot step, spring sideways on to the left foot, simultaneously raising the right foot backward. On the half-beat, insert the right toe beneath the left heel, projecting the left foot forward. Perform the right underfoot step in similar fashion, springing on to the right foot. In the second strain of *La Nizzarda*, 3 consecutive underfoot steps are made in one direction, finishing with joined feet. This constitutes an underfoot reprise (*ripresa in sotto piedi*).

The recacciata: This step occurs at the beginning of the third strain and occupies 2 beats. To make a left recacciata, hop on the right toe and kick backward with the left foot. At the *half*-beat, tap the ground with the left toe just behind the right heel. On the second beat, insert the left toe beneath the right heel, chasing the right foot forward, raised about three inches from the ground. Perform the right recacciata in similar fashion, hopping on the left toe and kicking back with the right.

LA NIZZARDA

Two Italian Dances: Passomezzo, La Nizzarda

del 𝄋

CHAPTER VIII

Two Balletti: Brando Alta Regina, La Barriera

BRANDO ALTA REGINA

THIS balleto, which, it may be observed, has diverged considerably from the *Branles* native to France (*Brando* being the Italian for *Branle*), is described by Cesare Negri, and is dedicated by him to the Queen of Spain, in these words: 'In gratia della Serenissima Donna Margherita, Regina di Spagna, Nostra Signora.' It is set for eight dancers, and was apparently performed in a masquerade held in honour of one of the periodical visits to Milan of the Queen Margherita, Consort of Filippo III. It is devised for four shepherds and four nymphs, appropriately attired, the shepherds carrying staves and the nymphs javelins. It is possible that this dance had been performed on previous occasions, but acquired its present title in celebration of this royal visit, which must have occurred soon after the accession of King Filippo III (1598). The name *Balletto* was applied originally by Domenichino de Piacenza to the suites of contrasting dance measures combined in one set dance which he initiated during his period of residence at the Court of Ferrara, early in the fifteenth century; and this type of dance may be regarded as the remote ancestor of the present day *Ballet*. The component parts of this *Balletto* consist of an *Intrada*, a *Contrapasso*, a *Saltarello* and a *Gagliarda*, the whole reiterated, and completed by a *Finale* and exit. I will for convenience describe this dance as though taking place on a stage and explain its various evolutions from the point of view of the dancers, so that there may be no confusion as to right and left turnings.

FIGURE I

Intrada

The dancers enter from centre back stage in double file, without holding hands, the nymphs to the right of their shepherds. The opening tune comprises 24 bars in duple time.

132

The double file advances down the centre with 2 broken singles (l.r.) and 1 broken double (l.), occupying 4 bars in all. They cast off (shepherd leftward and nymph to the right), followed by the others, and meet at back stage, forming a single row, in a concave half-circle (termed by Negri *mezza luna*), with the leading nymph and shepherd in the centre. This is accomplished with 2 broken singles (r.l.) and 1 broken double (r.). They perform a Grand Reverence of 4 bars' duration towards the spectators. The leading shepherd and his nymph, followed by the rest, advance hand in hand with 2 broken doubles (l.r.) occupying 4 bars. They continue their advance veering towards the left, the double file thus taking up its station broadside across the stage with the nymphs on the outside. This employs 2 more broken singles (l.r.) and 1 broken double (l.). Each dancer then describes a small circle with 2 broken singles (r.l.) and 1 broken double r., the nymphs circling clockwise and the shepherds anti-clockwise.

FIGURE II

Contrapasso

This strain consists of 18 bars. The singles and doubles used throughout are of the broken variety (*spezzati*). During the first 6 bars, the shepherds link right arms with their own nymphs, and they cross over into each other's places, with 1 broken double (l.), taking 2 bars. They then link left arms and cross back again with 2 broken singles (r.l.), taking another 2 bars. In the fifth and sixth bars, each dancer describes a circle with 1 more double (r.), the shepherds circling clockwise and the nymphs anti-clockwise, arriving back in their own places. This occupies bars five and six. During the second section of 6 bars, the double file of dancers divides into two halves, as follows: Shepherds Nos. 1 and 2 move leftwards with their own nymphs (whose right hand they hold in their own), making a sideways double. Simultaneously, shepherds 3 and 4, with their nymphs, move in the opposite direction. Shepherds 1 and 2 describe a circle (independently) moving anti-clockwise, with 2 singles and a double, while their nymphs similarly circle, but moving clockwise. The same actions are performed by couples 3 and 4, in the opposite direction (as in a looking-glass). During the remaining 6 bars, the partners all link left arms and perform the same actions as those occupying the first section of 6 bars. The double file remains divided into halves in preparation for figure III.

FIGURE III

Chain figure

This strain consists of 20 bars. During the first 10, couples 1 and 2 make a chain figure, while the third and fourth couples perform a ceremonial salutation. During the last 10 bars, the roles are reversed, the first two couples performing the salutation and the others making the chain figure, which they start from the opposite end of the file. The chain occupies 8 broken singles. During the first bar, the leader advances toward his nymph, to whom he gives his right hand, passing her with his right shoulder towards her and beginning with the left foot. As the lady moves into the place formerly occupied by her partner, the second shepherd turns towards her and, giving left hands, they pass into each other's places with a right broken single. Simultaneously the first shepherd has been passing the second nymph in the same manner. They continue thus until they arrive back in their own places. The first couple, having begun the chain, arrive home first and can describe a circle before landing in their own places. During the tenth bar, they remain stationary while the second couple describe a circle into their appointed places. During these 10 bars, the third and fourth couples proceed as follows: At bar one they step forward on to the flat of the right foot, and at bar two, advance the left toe an inch or two beyond the right foot, but with no weight on it. During the next 4 bars they perform the reverence, and during the remaining 4, 2 continenzas (l.r.). This brings us to the half of the strain.

During the second half, the roles are reversed, couples 1 and 2 making the formal salutations, and couples 3 and 4 the chain figure. This completes the strain of 20 bars. With the final chord, the ranks close up again, in readiness for figure IV.

FIGURE IV

Saltarello movement

This tune is in triple time, with the typical lilt of the saltarello. It contains 2 strains of 16 bars, both of which are repeated. The partners approach each other with a hopped broken double, occupying 4 bars. Linking right arms, they revolve twice, with 2 hopped broken doubles, occupying 8 bars, at the end of which they change places, with 1 more double, circling to the left. This brings us to the end of the first strain. As all the doubles in this figure are of the same character, I will henceforth omit the qualifying adjectives. During the repeat of the strain, they go through the same movements, but linking *left* arms and starting with the right foot. They return to their own places at the close. During the second strain, the partners approach each other with a left double, occupying 4 bars. Face to face, they make 2 sideways broken singles (r.l.), hopped on the final beat, occupying 4 bars. This is followed by 3 side-leaps (r.l.r.), closing with joined feet, and occupying 4 bars. During the last 4 bars, they make a diminished reprise to the right. If, however, this takes the opposite partners out of line with each other, they may return leftwards, when half-way through it. This brings us to the end of the second strain. During the repeat of the strain, the partners make a zigzag retreat with 4 sideways broken singles hopped on the last beat, in saltarello fashion (l.r.l.r.). This occupies 8 bars, and is followed by 3 side-leaps (l.r.l.), brought to a close by joined feet, taking 4 bars in all. The remaining 4 bars are filled by a diminished reprise to the left, returning towards the right if necessary for correct spacing.

FIGURE V

Gagliarda movement

Again the file of eight divides into two halves. Shepherds 1 and 2 link right arms with their partners, and revolve clockwise with 1 set of cinque-passi (l.r.) occupying 4 bars. They then link left arms, and revolve anti-clockwise with one more set of cinque-passi, occupying another 4 bars. This completes the first strain. The repeat is filled in the same manner with two sets of cinque-passi, the first set linking left arms, and revolving anti-clockwise, and the second linking right arms and revolving clockwise. Simultaneously, shepherds 3 and 4 perform a stately reverence of 4 bars' duration, and 1 cinque-passi (l.r.) occupying another 4, in company with their respective nymphs. During the repeat of the strain, they perform 2 sets of cinque-passi, in varied form, turning left and right. During the second strain and its repeat, couples 1 and 2 exchange roles with couples 3 and 4, performing the reverence, 1 cinque-passi and a varied set of cinque-passi, parading, while couples 3 and 4 perform the cinque-passi throughout, as done by the first two couples during the first strain. This completes the galliard figure.

FIGURE VI

Interlacing figure

This strain contains 16 bars in duple time, and employs the first tune in shortened form. It is filled by a kind of interlacing figure, in the first half of which, the two leaders (i.e. those at the head and the foot of the file), followed in each case by their companion shepherd, wind their way in and out between the four stationary nymphs. To make my directions clear, I will distinguish the four shepherds as A, B, C, and D. Speaking from the point of view of the dancers, A is the leader on the extreme left and D the leader on the right. A, advancing towards front stage, turns his right shoulder towards nymph No. 1 and passes round behind her back, followed by B. He then passes down between her and nymph No. 2, in front of whom he passes onwards. He next goes behind nymph No. 3, and passes down between her and No. 4. Deftly circling round No. 4, with his left shoulder towards her, he comes down (on his return journey) between her and No. 3, in front of whom he passes. Then, going up between her and No. 2, he circles round No. 2 and comes down into his own place, having passed between her and No. 1, and veering towards his right. The steps used in this interlacing figure consist entirely of 8 broken singles. B, who follows behind A, also finishes his journey, passing down between nymphs 2 and 1, and then into his own place, veering towards his left. Shepherds D and C follow the same process throughout, starting simultaneously from the opposite end of the file and first advancing towards front stage, so as to pass behind nymph No. 4 with their left shoulder towards her. At the finish of their return journey they pass down between nymphs 3 and 4, and so circle into their own places.

During the repeat of the strain, the shepherds remain stationary whilst the nymphs perform the same interlacing figure as that already done by their partners. Nymph No. 1 passes with her left shoulder towards partner.

FIGURE VII

Contrapasso

Figure VII employs tune No. 2 in a shortened form, consisting of 12 bars only, and follows on with a kind of coda, danced to tune No. 3, here reduced to 10 bars only.

During the first 6 bars, the dancers describe a circle to the left (each circling independently anti-clockwise) with 1 broken double (l.) occupying 2 bars, 2 broken singles (r.l.), occupying another 2 bars, and 1 more broken double (r.), which completes the first half of the strain. During the second half, they repeat the same series of steps, circling clockwise. This completes the strain of 12 bars.

Coda

In the ten-bar coda which Negri attaches to his seventh figure, the double file of dancers separates once again into two sets of four. Both leaders start a chain figure (each within his own set), containing 6 hopped broken singles. Leader A advances toward his own nymph with 1 broken single (l.), giving her his right hand, and they pass into each other's places. He then gives his left hand to nymph No. 2 and they pass each other in the same manner; and so he continues. Having arrived back, after having given his hand four times in all, he circles leftwards, regaining his own place, where he remains stationary during the sixth bar. B, who follows him at 1 bar's distance (having remained stationary during bar one), gives his left hand to nymph No. 1, making a *right* broken single. He will thus arrive home with 1 bar left, in which to circle neatly into his own place. During the remaining 4 bars, the two shepherds take their respective nymphs by the right hand, and they revolve to the right, with 2 broken doubles, at the close of which, taking their partner's *left* hand in their own right, they perform a half-reverence (*presto*), ranging themselves two by two, in readiness for the passeggio which starts the succeeding figure.

The other four dancers, headed by D, perform their chain figure simultaneously at the opposite end. Leader D, beginning with a right hopped broken single, gives his left hand to his own nymph, and so conducts the chain figure in the opposite direction. During the last 4 bars, the partners, holding left hands, revolve leftwards.

FIGURE VIII

Saltarello

This figure is performed to tune No. 4 with repeats, and is in saltarello rhythm. During the first strain the dancers, hand in hand, follow the leading couple round leftwards towards back stage and up the centre, with 6 hopped doubles (taking 4 bars each). They release hands and, turning face to face, make 4 balzetti (l.r.l.r.), occupying 4 bars in all, and 1 hopped double, circling independently clockwise. This occupies the first 16-bar strain and its repeat. During the second strain, the partners, holding right hands (shoulder high), revolve twice to the right, with 2 hopped broken doubles (r.l.). Releasing hands, they turn face to face and perform 2 dotted singles (*puntate*), occupying 2 bars each (r.l.), in retreat, and 1 hopped double, advancing towards each other. This completes the second strain once. During the repeat of the second strain, the same series of steps is repeated, beginning with the left foot, and revolving anti-clockwise.

FIGURE IX

Figure IX uses the same music as that of the preceding figure, and takes the form of a passeggio, clockwise round the stage. It employs 16 broken doubles which occupy the entire tune with its repeats. During the first two doubles the dancers advance. During the next two, each shepherd takes the left hand of the nymph in his right (holding it lightly by the finger-tips, above her head), and circles round her clockwise. The nymph meanwhile remains stationary. During the next 4 bars, they advance with two doubles, and then the nymph circles round her partner with 2 more doubles, anti-clockwise, holding her partner's right hand in her left. So they continue to alternate their advance and their circling, turn and turn about until the end of the tune. This closes the saltarello movement.

FIGURE X

This figure is performed to tune No. 5, played twice. The partners release hands, and the leading shepherd and nymph cast off to left and right, followed by the others of their respective files. The leading pair meet in the centre at the back of the stage, flanked by their followers so as to form a hollow curve (*mezza luna*). This occupies 4 broken doubles and fills the first strain of 8 bars and its repeat. During the second strain of 8 bars (with no repeat), the dancers make 4 sideways broken singles (shepherds l.r.l.r., nymphs r.l.r.l.). The dancers continue to face forward (*mezza luna*). Tune No. 5 is now repeated with both strains played once only. During the first strain, they perform 2 continenzas occupying 4 bars (shepherds l.r. and nymphs r.l.). This is followed by 3 side-leaps, closing with

137

joined feet, occupying 4 bars (shepherds l.r.l. and nymphs r.l.r.). This completes the first strain. During the second strain, the dancers make 2 diminished reprises, taking 4 bars in all (shepherds l.r., nymphs r.l.), followed by a reverence towards the spectators of 4 bars' duration. This completes the second strain.

Finale

The music of the finale consists of 2 strains in duple time. The first strain comprises 12 bars and is repeated. The second strain comprises 16 bars with no repeat. The music is in duple time. The leading shepherd and nymph, followed by the others, advance towards front stage with 4 broken doubles (l.r.l.r.), taking 8 bars in all, and 4 broken singles, taking 4 bars. This completes the first strain. During the repeat, they cast off to left and right and, meeting at back stage, they lead up the middle again, using the same series of steps. This completes the repeat of the first strain. At the second strain the partners turn face to face and perform a reverence of 4 bars. They face forward again and the file of dancers, veering round to the right, circle the stage with broken doubles. The shepherds then lead their partners to a seat with a parting reverence. If preferred, the dancers may instead make their exit.

The order of the steps

FIGURE I

Intrada

Duple time.

2 broken singles l.r.	advancing	4 bars
1 broken double l.		
2 broken singles r.l.	casting off	4 bars
1 broken double r.		
Reverence		4 bars
2 broken doubles l.r., advancing		4 bars
2 broken singles l.r.		4 bars
1 broken double l.		
2 broken singles r.l.	turning left across stage	4 bars
1 broken double		
		24 bars

FIGURE II

1 broken double l.	crossing over and back	
2 broken singles r.l.	circling left	6 bars
1 broken double r.		
1 sideways double l.	file divides in two halves	
2 broken singles r.l.	circling l.	6 bars
1 broken double r.	circling r.	
1 broken double l.	crossing over and back	
2 broken singles r.l.	circling l.	6 bars
1 broken double r.		
		18 bars

FIGURE III

(Chain)

First four: 8 broken singles, and circle into place	10 bars
Second four: 1 dotted single r.	2 bars
Simultaneously { Reverence	4 bars
{ 2 continenzas l.r.	4 bars
	10 bars
The two sets of four reverse their roles	10 bars
Total	20 bars

FIGURE IV

Saltarello

Triple time.

First strain (partners remain face to face):

1 hopped broken double l., advancing	4 bars
2 hopped broken doubles r.l., revolving and changing places	8 bars
1 hopped broken double r., circling left	4 bars
(Repeat)	16 bars
Repeat same figure returning to places	16 bars

139

Second strain:

1 hopped broken double l., sideways	4 bars
2 hopped broken singles r.l., sideways	4 bars
3 side-leaps and join feet r.l.r.l.	4 bars
1 diminished reprise r.	4 bars
(Repeat)	16 bars
4 hopped broken singles l.r.l.r., retreating	8 bars
3 side-leaps and join feet l.r.l.r.	4 bars
1 diminished reprise l.	4 bars
	16 bars

FIGURE V

Gagliarda

First strain:

First four dancers.	Partners link arms and revolve clockwise and anti-clockwise with 4 sets of cinque-passi	16 bars
Second four dancers.	Grand Reverence and 1 cinque-passi	8 bars
	2 sets of cinque-passi (*raccortati*)	8 bars
		16 bars

Second strain:

The roles of the two sets of four dancers are reversed	16 bars
	Total 32 bars

FIGURE VI

Interlacing figure

Duple time.

8 broken doubles. Shepherds move, nymphs stationary	16 bars
(Repeat) 8 broken doubles. Nymphs move, shepherds stationary	16 bars
	32 bars

FIGURE VII

Contrapasso

1 broken double l., circling left	2 bars
2 broken singles r.l., revolving together	2 bars
1 broken double l., circling	2 bars
Same series of steps repeated, using opposite feet	6 bars
	12 bars

Coda

The file again divides in two, each set making a simultaneous chain figure.

6 broken singles l.r.l.r.l.r. (other set, r.l.r.l.r.l.)	6 bars
2 broken doubles, revolving clockwise	2 bars
2 broken doubles, revolving anti-clockwise	2 bars
	10 bars

FIGURE VIII

Saltarello

Triple time.

First strain:

6 hopped doubles; leading round and up centre	24 bars
4 balzetti (partners face to face) l.r.l.r.	4 bars
1 hopped double l., circling left	4 bars
	32 bars

Second strain:

2 hopped doubles r.l., revolving right	8 bars
2 dotted singles r.l., retreating	4 bars
1 hopped double r., advancing	4 bars
2 hopped doubles l.r., revolving left	8 bars
2 dotted singles l.r., retreating	4 bars
1 hopped double l., advancing	4 bars
	32 bars

FIGURE IX

Repeat of saltarello

16 doubles round the stage clockwise; intermittent circling round partner	64 bars

FIGURE X

Gagliarda

First strain twice:	
4 doubles l.r.l.r., casting off	16 bars
Second strain once:	
4 singles l.r.l.r. (Nymphs, r.l.r.l.)	8 bars
First strain once:	
2 continenzas l.r. (Nymphs, r.l.)	4 bars
3 side-leaps and join feet l.r.l.r. (Nymphs, r.l.r.l.)	4 bars
Second strain once:	
2 diminished reprises	4 bars
Reverence	4 bars
	40 bars

Nymphs use opposite feet throughout this figure.

Finale

Duple time. Lead up centre.

First strain twice:	
4 broken doubles l.r.l.r.	8 bars
4 broken singles l.r.l.r.	4 bars
	12 bars
4 broken doubles l.r.l.r., cast off	8 bars
4 broken singles l.r.l.r., lead up centre	4 bars
	12 bars
Second strain once:	
Reverence	4 bars
Turn right and circle stage, with 4 broken doubles l.r.l.r.	8 bars
Lead partner to seat with 4 broken singles	4 bars
Congé on final chord	16 bars

142

Two Balletti: Brando Alta Regina, La Barriera

Although there is not a great variety in the type of steps introduced in this balletto, their manner of performance differs according to the contrasting dance rhythms employed. The first three tunes use the reverence, continenzas, broken singles and doubles.

The reverence: This occupies 4 bars in duple time. On the first beat of bar one, advance the left foot a few inches, and hold it there throughout the bar, with the toe well pointed, resting the weight on the right foot. During bar two, draw the left foot back behind the right. At bar three, transfer the weight on to the left foot, bending the knee and inclining the head and body. At bar 4, transfer the weight back to the right foot, and join the left foot to it, rising on the toes and raising the head and body. Sink the heels at the close.

Two continenzas: These occupy 2 bars each in duple time. To make a left continenza, step sideways on the flat of the left foot, bending the knee outwards. At the half-bar, rise on the toes. At bar two, join the right foot to the left, and sink the left heel. The hip should be advanced slightly in the direction in which the dancer is moving.

Perform the right continenza in similar fashion.

The broken singles (spezzati): These take 1 bar each. For a left broken single, in duple time, step forward on the flat of the left foot. At the half-beat, bring up the right foot to the heel of the left, rising on the toes, and raising the left foot forward. On the second beat, bring down the left foot (advanced about two inches) on the flat of the foot. Make the right broken single in similar fashion.

The broken doubles: These take 2 bars each in duple time. On the first beat of the first bar, step forward on the left toe, and on the second beat, step forward on the right toe. On the first beat of bar two, step forward on the flat of the left foot, and at the half-beat, bring up the right foot to the heel of the left, rising on the toes and raising the left foot forward. On the second beat, bring down the left foot (advanced about two inches) on the flat of the foot. Perform the right broken double in similar fashion.

FIGURE IV

Saltarello movement

This tune is in triple time. The steps employed throughout the first strain are hopped broken doubles. The music goes at a lively pace.

Hopped broken doubles: These occupy 4 bars each. On the first beat of bar one, step on the ball of the left foot, and on the third beat, hop on it. During the second bar, perform the same actions with the right foot. On the first beat of bar three, step forward on the flat of the left foot, bending the knee outward, and on the third beat, bring up the right toe behind the left heel, rising on the toes. On the first beat of bar four, step forward again on the flat of the left foot, and on the third beat, hop on the left toe. Perform the right hopped broken double in similar fashion, beginning with the right foot.

143

The saltarello tune, in addition to the hopped doubles, also employs the hopped broken single (named in the fifteenth century *passo Brabante*), the side-leaps (*trabuchetti*), and the diminished reprise.

Hopped broken singles (*seguiti spezzati in saltino*): These occupy 2 bars each in triple time. On the first beat of bar one, step forward on the flat of the left foot, bending the knee, and on the third beat, bring the right toe level with the left heel, rising on the toes. On the first beat of bar two, step forward again on the flat of the left foot, bending the knee a little and rising again. On the third beat, hop on the left toe, raising the right foot forward in readiness for the right single. Perform the right hopped broken single in similar fashion.

The side-leaps (*trabuchetti*): To make a left side-leap, spring sideways on to the left toe with well-straightened knees and raise the right foot forward in front of the left, with the toe well pointed. Perform the right side-leap in similar fashion, and if a third is required spring back again on to the left toe, raising the right in front. Then at the fourth bar, lower the right foot beside the left in the first position. Each side-leap takes 1 bar in the saltarello movement.

The diminished reprise: This consists of a sideways movement, made by the alternate opening and closing of the toes and heels. To move leftwards, first move the left heel and right toe in that direction, and then the left toe and right heel. Make as many of these double twists as the time allows.

TUNE NO. V

The Galliard

The cinque-passi revolving: Negri describes many ways of performing the *cinque-passi*, some of which are extremely complicated. As used, however, in this balletto, the simplest kind, namely, that used for counterpassing, is indicated. Each set occupies 4 bars. The partners link right arms first, and revolve clockwise. On the first beat of bar one, hop on the right foot and kick the left foot forward, instantly lowering it at the half-beat. On the second beat, hop on the left foot, and kick the right foot forward, lowering it at the half-beat. On the third beat, hop on the right again, and kick with the left, lowering it as before. On the first beat of bar two, hop once more on the left and kick with the right, lowering it at the half-beat in front of the left. Now comes the cadenza, which constitutes the fifth step. On the second beat, bend the knees and spring into the air. Scooping the left foot forward and quickly drawing it back, alight on the third beat of bar two in the third position right. Continue to revolve in the same direction with the other half of the set, hopping first on the left foot and kicking with the right. This brings us to the half of the strain. During the second half the same series is repeated, linking left arms and revolving anti-clockwise. Repeat the same formula during the second strain.

Two Balletti: Brando Alta Regina, La Barriera

The reverence: The reverence which follows is similar to that performed in figure III, but goes at a faster tempo. The variation with reduced steps (*cinque-passi raccortati*) in the second strain goes as follows:

Turn right shoulder to partner, and, on the first beat, perform a sliding step on the right foot; on the second beat, make a left zoppetto, hopping on the right foot and raising the left foot in front (the knee a little bent), bringing it down on the third beat in front of the right. During the second bar, bend both knees outward, then rise on the toes and on the third beat make a half-turn right, so as to present the left shoulder to partner. During bar three, step forward on the left foot, and during the second and third beats make a right zoppetto, hopping on the left foot. In the fourth bar, make the left cadenza, bending on the first beat, then rising in the air as you scoop the left foot forward and draw it back again, alighting on the third beat, in the third position right. Repeat left.

The stationary galliard step (passo largo fermato in galliarda): Standing on the flat of the left foot with the right foot joined, bend the knee and slide the right foot round in a semicircle, placing it in front of the left in the third position, rising on the toes with straightened knees. This occupies 1 beat. Perform the second step in similar fashion, by sliding the left foot round on the first beat of bar five.

We now arrive at figure VI, whose steps consist entirely of broken doubles in duple time, as described in connection with figures I, II, and III.

FIGURE VII AND CODA

These two movements are in duple time. The first contains the same singles and doubles as those described in figures I, II, and III. The second part uses the tune belonging to figure III: and its steps consist of broken singles taking 1 bar each, and with a little hop at the close of each single, in saltarello style.

FIGURES VIII AND IX

These two figures are danced to the fourth tune, which is a saltarello, and consequently contain only hopped broken singles and doubles, as described in the previous saltarello figure.

FIGURE X

This figure, though danced to the galliard tune, employs only broken singles (without hops), continenzas, side-leaps and diminished reprises, closing with a Grand Reverence.

The diminished reprise (ripresa minuita): This consists of a sideways movement made by the opening and closing of the toes and heels, alternating the true first position with the false first position wherein the toes are joined and the heels parted. To move leftwards,

145

first move the left heel and right toe to the left. The opposite proceeding travels to the right.

Finale

This is in duple time and contains only smooth singles and doubles, performed as in figures I, II, and III.

BRANDO ALTA REGINA

II CONTRAPASSO

III CHAIN FIGURE

IV SALTARELLO

Two Balletti: Brando Alta Regina, La Barriera

V GAGLIARDA

VI DOUBLE INTERLACING (Shepherds)

(Nymphs)

VII CONTRAPASSO

VIII and IX SALTARELLO

Two Balletti: Brando Alta Regina, La Barriera

Da Capo (with repeats)

X GAGLIARDA

FINALE

LA BARRIERA

This ancient dance, whose Spanish name is *El Torneo*, represents a mimic Tournament, and is doubtless of medieval origin. The earliest known version appears in the *Manuscrit de Marie de Bourgogne* (*c.* 1450), being the last dance in that famous collection. Therein, it is arranged for three dancers, under the title *Bęaulté de Castille*. Caroso gives us four versions in all; and Negri yet another. Of the various tunes which exist for this dance (all based upon trumpet-calls and flourishes), I find that of Caroso particularly attractive. I have therefore chosen that one for inclusion in the present volume.

In Caroso's second treatise (*Nobilita dei Dame*), from which this *Barriera* is drawn, he has invented some fantastic names for certain groups of steps. These I propose to ignore, merely detailing the steps in question, with their individual names.

LA BARRIERA

Two Balletti: Brando Alta Regina, La Barriera

Barriera Nuova

The six dancers, consisting of three cavaliers and three ladies, arrange themselves in a circle, with each lady on her partner's right. The first seven figures are all danced to the same tune, which contains 24 bars, and is played seven times in succession.

FIGURE I

The dancers form a fairly wide ring. During the first 8 bars they perform the reverence of 4 bars' duration (*Riverenza longa*), followed by two continenzas occupying 2 bars each. During these 8 opening bars, the partners turn face to face. These salutations being concluded, they turn to face the centre of the circle. Taking hands, they now circle leftwards, with two slow steps (l.r.), taking 1 bar each, and 1 ordinary double (l.), taking 2 bars. This is followed by 2 more singles (r.l.) and 1 double (r.). They release hands, and each cavalier turns to face the lady on his *left*. They perform 2 continenzas (l.r.) and the reverence. This brings us to the end of the strain.

FIGURE II

The dancers (in a circle) make a zigzag advance towards centre, with 2 slow dotted singles (*puntate grave*) to left and right, occupying 4 bars in all. The partners turn face to face and circle round each other clockwise with 4 stealthy steps (l.r.l.r.) as though stalking. This takes another 4 bars. Arriving back in their own places, and facing each other, they make an ordinary double sideways to the left and another to the right, thus moving in contrary motion. This occupies 4 bars and brings us to the half of the strain. During the next 4 bars they make 1 slow continenza of 4 bars' duration (l.). This is followed by 2 underfoot steps (*sotto'piedi*) and 1 hopped broken single (all to the right), occupying 4 bars. The figure comes to a close with 3 underfoot steps to the left and 1 side-leap (l.), closing with joined feet, occupying the last 4 bars of the strain.

FIGURE III

Each cavalier turns towards the lady on his left and they repeat the same figure, beginning with the right foot, and circling round each other with their stalking steps, anti-clockwise.

FIGURE IV

The cavaliers turn to face their own partners and, holding right hands, they make 1 forward dotted single (*puntata*) with the left foot, and 1 quick broken double in retreat with the right. This occupies 4 bars in all. They release hands with a quick half-reverence, and during the next 4 bars they circle round each other as in the preceding figure with 4 stealthy steps as though stalking, keeping their faces turned towards each other. Once more face to face in their own places, they make a sideways double to the left, taking 2 bars, followed by a diminished reprise towards the right, occupying 2 bars. This is followed by a slow continenza (l.) of 4 bars' length. The strain concludes with the 2 underfoot steps and 1 hopped broken single (all towards the right) and the 3 underfoot steps and 1 side-leap (all towards the left).

FIGURE V

Each cavalier turns towards the lady on his left, and they repeat the same figure, beginning with the right foot and circling anti-clockwise.

FIGURE VI

The ladies remain stationary while the cavaliers perform this figure. Each approaches his partner with 4 sideways broken singles made in zigzag fashion (l.r.l.r.). This occupies 4 bars. They then retreat with a dotted broken single (l.), turning a little towards the left, at the close of which each cavalier removes his hat with a half-reverence (r.). He then makes a similar step with the right foot, again removing his hat with a half-reverence. These 2 steps occupy another four bars. During the next 4 bars, the cavaliers make 2 side-leaps (l.r.), facing partner, and 1 underfoot step (l.), retreating sideways, followed by another side-leap (l.). This occupies 4 bars and is followed by the same series of steps to the right, occupying another 4 bars. There remain another 8 bars, during which the reverence is made first by the cavaliers towards their partners, and then reciprocated by the ladies.

FIGURE VII

The ladies facing their partners repeat the foregoing figure. Naturally they have no hats to remove during the broken dotted singles, but make instead a graceful gesture with the arms, which they draw backwards on the side of the foot which starts the movement.

FIGURE VIII

This figure is performed to the second tune, which is in triple time. The dancers face toward the centre of the circle, all holding hands. They circle leftwards with 2 sideways steps, taking 1 bar each (l.r.), treading lightly on the ball of the foot on the first beat of the bar, and hopping on the third beat. In making the second step, they pass the right foot behind the left. During the third and fourth bars, they make a sideways broken double (l.). During the next 4 bars they repeat this series of steps, beginning with the right foot, and circling to the right. Still holding hands, they make, during the ninth and tenth bars, 2 dotted singles, one advancing towards centre (l.) and the other retreating (r.). These steps are made on the flat of the foot in a challenging manner, but rising on the toes, as the other foot joins the stepping one. During the eleventh and twelfth bars (still hand in hand) the dancers make a concerted rush towards the centre of the circle, using tiny half-steps in rapid succession on the toes. As they all meet in the centre, they raise their joined hands. During the next 4 bars, they make 4 quick broken singles, occupying 1 bar each (l.r.l.r.), in *retreat*. As they make these steps, they turn (obliquely) alternately to left and right. This brings us to the end of bar sixteen. They now release hands, and the partners turn face to face. During bars seventeen and eighteen, they make a left continenza and follow this with a right underfoot step and a right side-leap. This occupies another 2 bars. The remaining 4 bars of the strain are filled with 3 left underfoot steps and a left cadenza, alighting with feet joined in the first position.

FIGURE IX

The foregoing figure is repeated beginning with the right foot and circling first to the right. From bar seventeen onwards, each cavalier turns face to face with the lady on his left, and they complete the figure in this fashion, using throughout the opposite foot to that employed in the preceding figure.

FIGURE X

Saltarello (third tune)

The dancers perform 4 sideways broken singles, *presto* (l.r.l.r.), facing centre. This occupies 4 bars. During the next 4 bars, they clap hands four times, each cavalier clapping first his left hand on his partner's right hand, and then his right hand on the left hand of the lady on his other side. This brings us to the half of the strain. During the remaining 8 bars, they perform the same actions, beginning with the right foot and clapping hands first with the other dancer (cavalier's right hand on the other lady's left, and then left hand on his partner's right). There follow 8 bars in duple time, during which the dancers face towards centre and perform 2 continenzas (l.r.) and a reverence of 4 bars.

Finale

Sciolta in Gagliarda

The music of the Finale contains 24 bars.

This is a chain figure in which the dancers first give their right hands to their own partners, and after passing each other with one broken double, they each give their left hands to the next person, passing on with another broken double, and so they continue until they have given their hand six times and performed 6 broken doubles, occupying 12 bars in all. By this time the partners will be back in their original places. Facing centre, they perform 2 continenzas of 2 bars each, followed by 2 dotted singles in retreat, taking another 4 bars. During the remaining 4 bars each cavalier takes his lady's hand and they perform the reverence of 4 bars. This concludes the balletto.

The order of the steps

FIGURE I

Reverence to partner	4 bars
2 continenzas l.r.	4 bars
2 slow steps l.r., sideways to left	2 bars
1 ordinary double l.r.l., sideways to left	2 bars
Reverence to lady on left side	4 bars
2 continenzas r.l.	4 bars
2 slow steps r.l., sideways to right	2 bars
1 ordinary double r.l.r., sideways to right	2 bars
	24 bars

FIGURE II

2 dotted singles, advancing towards centre	4 bars
4 slow steps (partners circling face to face)	4 bars
2 sideways ordinary doubles l.r.	4 bars
1 slow continenza l.	4 bars
2 underfoot steps and 1 broken single r.	4 bars
3 underfoot steps and 1 side-leap l., join feet	4 bars
	24 bars

FIGURE III

Same figure repeated, beginning right foot and turning towards lady on left side.

FIGURE IV

Turn to face own partner.

1 dotted single l.; 1 broken double r.	4 bars
4 slow steps, circling round each other	4 bars
1 sideways double l.	2 bars
1 diminished reprise r.	2 bars
1 slow continenza	4 bars
2 underfoot steps and 1 broken single r.	4 bars
3 underfoot steps and 1 side-leap l., join feet	4 bars
	24 bars

FIGURE V

Repeat same figure, beginning with right foot and turning towards lady on left side.

FIGURE VI

Ladies remain stationary.

Man approaches partner with 4 broken singles, zigzag	4 bars
1 dotted single retreating l., 1 ditto r.	4 bars
2 side-leaps l.r.; 1 underfoot step l., one side-leap l.	4 bars
Same series of steps, beginning right foot	4 bars
Reverence towards lady	4 bars
Lady makes reverence in return.	4 bars
	24 bars

FIGURE VII

Men remain stationary.

Ladies repeat figure in their turn	24 bars

FIGURE VIII

Dancers face centre, holding hands.	
They circle with 2 hopped steps l.r. and 1 broken double l.	4 bars
They repeat same to right	4 bars
2 dotted singles towards centre l.r., presto	2 bars
Scorsa towards centre	2 bars
4 quick broken singles, retreating	4 bars
1 continenza l.	2 bars
1 underfoot step; 1 side-leap r.	2 bars
3 underfoot steps l.; cadenza l.	4 bars
	24 bars

FIGURE IX

Repeat same using opposite foot.

FIGURE X

4 sideways broken singles, presto	4 bars
Clap hands	4 bars
Repeat same actions, beginning right foot	8 bars

Duple time

2 continenzas l.r. and reverence	8 bars
	24 bars

Finale in Gagliarda

6 broken doubles in chain figure	12 bars
2 continenzas l.r.	4 bars
2 dotted singles in retreat l.r.	4 bars
Reverence	4 bars
	24 bars

Two Balletti: Brando Alta Regina, La Barriera

Grand Reverence (*Riverenza longa*): Stand with the weight resting on the right foot, and at bar one, advance the left foot a few inches beyond the right, with the toe well pointed, and no weight on it. At bar two, draw back the left foot a little way behind the right, inclining the head and body. At bar three, transfer the weight on to the left foot, bending the knee. At bar four, restore the weight on to the right foot and simultaneously join the left foot to the right, rising on the toes, and raising the head and body. Sink the heels at the close.

The continenzas: These take 2 bars each. At bar one, step sideways on the flat of the left foot, bending the knee and swaying slightly towards the left. At bar two, rising on the toes, join the right foot to the left in the third position right. Sink the heels at the close. Make the right continenza in similar fashion, moving towards the right.

The slow steps (*passi grave*): Step suavely on the flat of the foot, rising on to the ball of the foot at the close. It produces a pleasing effect, if the head is turned in the direction of the stepping foot. These steps occupy 1 bar each.

The quick steps (*passi minimi*): These take half a bar each in duple time, and are made lightly on the toes.

The ordinary singles (*passi semibreve*): These occupy 1 bar each. On the first beat, step on the flat of the foot, and at the half-bar, join the other foot to it, rising on the toes.

The ordinary double (*seguito ordinario*): The step which Caroso names thus, consists of 2 quick steps, made on the toes, occupying 1 bar together, and 1 slow step made on the flat of the foot (rising again at the half-bar) and occupying the second bar. The dancer should sway a little during the slow step towards the side of the stepping foot.

The underfoot step (*sotto piede*): This step may be used singly or in groups. To make a left underfoot step, leap sideways on to the ball of the left foot, kicking the right foot backwards. At the half-bar insert the right toe beneath the left heel, projecting the left foot forward. When a succession of such steps are made, this constitutes an underfoot reprise, at whose close the raised foot is lowered beside the other foot. For the right underfoot step, hop sideways on to the right foot, and insert the left toe beneath the right heel. The series of underfoot steps and side-leaps which form a kind of chorus at the close of many of the figures, should be performed, according to Caroso, with the legs straight and taut. For this reason he applies the name destice thereto. The effect, to my mind, suggests a galloping horse.

Dotted singles: At the first bar, step obliquely forward, or back. At bar two, bend both knees, and at the half-bar, join up the other foot, rising on the toes.

Broken singles: These are performed as described for the first three figures of Brando Alta Regina.

The steps above described belong to the first seven figures, which are all danced to the first tune, played seven times over. The eighth figure is of a different character. It is termed by Caroso *Folla*, pronounced *follia* in Spanish, which name was formerly applied to the mêlée in a tournament. The music is in triple time and goes at a brisk pace. I will therefore describe the steps in the manner suitable to this kind of rhythm.

FIGURE VIII

The mêlée

Hopped steps: These occupy 1 bar each. On the first beat, step sideways on the ball of the left foot, and on the third beat, hop on it. As the dancers are circling, the second step (which follows on the right foot) will be passed behind the left foot. When the dancers reverse their direction, the first step (on the right foot) is followed by one made on the left foot, passed behind the right.

Quick sideways doubles: Step leftwards on the ball of the left foot, on the first beat of bar one, and on the third beat, pass the right foot behind the left. On the first beat of bar two, step again sideways with the left foot, and on the third beat, hop on it. Make the right double in similar fashion, beginning with the right foot.

Quick dotted singles (puntate preste): These take 1 bar each, in triple time. On the first beat, step forward on the left foot (for a left puntata) and on the second beat bend the knees. On the third beat, join the right foot to the left, in the first position, rising on the toes. In this figure, the step would be made in the manner of a challenge, putting the advancing foot down smartly. The retreating single which follows is also made in a bold manner. In making these 2 steps, turn the left shoulder towards the centre of the ring.

The passage in half-steps (scorsa): This is made on the tips of the toes with the left shoulder turned obliquely towards centre. The steps should be made very small, and as many made as can be fitted into the 2 bars, so as to portray an impetuous rush into the fray. The left foot steps first, and then the right toe is brought up to the middle of the left foot for the second half-step.

Quick broken singles in triple time: These take 1 bar each, and are made in retreat, zigzag fashion, turning to left and right. To make the left single, step back sideways on the flat of the left foot and on the second beat, rising on the toes, join the right foot to the left. On the third beat, step again sideways on the left toe, and make a quick half-turn right on it, so as to be ready to start the second sideways single with the right foot. Four singles are made in the retreat after the forward rush to centre.

The steps of the gagliarda figure consist principally of quick broken doubles. These are performed in a light and agile manner. Each double occupies 2 bars in triple time. The pace of the gagliarda is, however, rather slower than that of the saltarello. On the first beat of bar one, step forward on the left toe in a springy manner. On the second beat, step forward on the flat of the right foot, and on the third beat, rise on the toes. On the first beat of bar two, step forward on the flat of the left foot, and on the second beat, rising

160

on the toes, insert the right toe beneath the left heel, projecting the left foot forward, raised a few inches from the ground. On the third beat, spring lightly on to the flat of the left foot, rising again at the close, in preparation for the right double, which is made in similar fashion, beginning with the right foot.

The slow dotted singles: These occupy 2 bars each. At bar one, step forward obliquely on the flat of the left foot. On the first beat of bar two, bend the knees outwards, and on the third beat, rising on the toes, join the left foot to the right. Sway the hip slightly in the direction of the first stepping foot in each single.

The reverence: This will occupy 4 bars and should be performed as in the opening bars of figure I.

LA BARRIERA

To be played 7 times.

161

Two Balletti: Brando Alta Regina, La Barriera

PART IV GAGLIARDA

CHAPTER IX

Two Hundred Years of Dancing

HAVING brought to the notice of my readers some of the interesting and beautiful court dances of Spain and Italy which flourished during the fifteenth and sixteenth centuries, I feel that this work would yet be incomplete without the inclusion of one of the earliest *Balli* devised by their inventor, Domenichino of Piacenza. In the one surviving copy of this treatise, the second half is devoted exclusively to these *Balli*. The anonymous writer who has preserved this work for posterity tells us that both the music (with one exception) and the choreography were composed by 'lo Spectabile et egregio cavagliero Misser Domenico da piasenza'. From among the thirteen *Balli* accompanied by music, I have chosen one whose melodies were harmonized by Arnold Dolmetsch. It is named *La Gelosia* (spelt in the original treatise *La Giloxia*).

LA GELOSIA

This is a dance for six people, three men and three ladies. I will, for convenience, describe it as though taking place on a stage, using the terms *right* and *left* as from the point of view of the dancers.

FIGURE I

Intrada

The three couples enter from the centre in double file and perform an intrada with slow saltarello steps occupying 8 bars of music, with 6 beats to the bar. Veering first to the right, they then turn leftwards and take up their position across the front of the stage, with a distance of 3 paces between the couples. The partners turn face to face.

FIGURE II

Quadernaria measure

This figure occupies 12 bars of music in duple time. The ladies remain stationary throughout. The leading man approaches his partner and, with his right shoulder turned towards her, circles round her, making 3 doubles, occupying 1 bar each. At the fourth bar, touching her right hand with his own, he makes a reverence of 4 beats. During the next 4 bars, he goes up between the first and second ladies and, passing behind the second lady, comes down between her and the third lady, making 3 more doubles, after which, turning to face the second lady and touching her right hand, he performs a reverence of 4 beats. Releasing her hand, he turns towards the third lady and, circling round her, with his left shoulder turned towards her, he makes 3 more doubles. During the final bar, he turns to face her and, touching her right hand with his own, performs a reverence of 4 beats. Having explained the movements of the leading man throughout this figure, I must now return to the beginning in order to describe the actions of the second and third men.

During the first 6 bars, the second man remains stationary. During bars seven and eight, he makes a sideways double leftwards so as to take up his position opposite to the first lady, towards whom he then makes a reverence in accordance with the procedure of the leader. He remains stationary during the rest of the figure. The third man remains stationary throughout the first 10 bars. During the eleventh and twelfth bars he makes a sideways double (l.), so as to stand opposite to the second lady, towards whom he makes a reverence. Thus the leading man, who started at the head of the dance, is now at the foot, opposite to the third lady.

FIGURE III

Piva

The *Piva* was originally a peasant dance whose light, springing steps, interspersed with hops, were performed to the accompaniment of the bagpipe. Short strains of piva were later introduced into the *Balli* as a pleasing contrast to the more sedate measures. The Italians, both in their music and in their dances, delighted in these startling transitions in style and tempo.

The couple at the head of the dance describe a circle (the man circling leftwards and the lady to the right). This is performed with 3 hopped singles (l.r.l.) and joined feet, and occupies 2 bars. They halt; and the middle couple in their turn perform the same circle. This brings us to the end of the strain. In the first 2 bars of the repeat, the third couple perform their circle in like manner. During the third and fourth bars, the respective partners all simultaneously cross over into each other's places, with 3 hopped singles (l.r.l.), giving right hands. On the final beat, they make a half-turn. The strain is played a third time. During the first 2 bars, they return to their own places with 3 hopped singles (r.l.r.), giving left hands, and making a half-turn at the close. The last 2 bars are filled by another circle performed simultaneously, the men circling to the right and the ladies to the left. During the section for *congé*, the partners make a reverence towards each other.

It is then explained that, since the man who was the leader is now at the foot of the dance, the whole ballo must be performed a second and third time, so that all three men may finally regain their original partners, the implication being that all *gelosia* will thus be ended.

HOW TO PERFORM THE STEPS

The saltarello step: This occupies 1 bar of 6 beats. To make a left saltarello step (*passo Brabante*), step forward on the flat of the left foot, bending the knee; on the third beat, bring up the right toe level with the left heel, rising on the toes with straightened knees. On the fourth beat, step forward again on the flat of the left foot, bending the knee, and at the sixth beat, hop on the left toe, raising the right foot forward ready for the following step.

The double: Each double occupies 1 bar of 4 beats. To make a left double, step forward on the flat of the left foot, bending the knee. On the second beat, step forward with the right foot, rising on the toes of both feet. On the third beat, step again on the flat of the left foot, bending the knee, and swaying slightly leftwards. On the fourth beat, join the right foot to the left, in the first position, and rise on the toes of both feet. Sink the heels at the close.

The Piva steps: The *Piva*, being a rapid dance, usually employs two steps (plain or ornamented) to a bar. Only one kind of step is used in this ballo. There are 6 beats to the bar. On the first beat, step on the left toe, and on the third beat, hop on it, raising the right foot forward. On the fourth beat, step on the right foot, and on the sixth beat, hop on it, raising the left foot forward. The toe should be well pointed. When the couples change places by means of 3 hopped singles (l.r.l.), the raised foot (r.) on the fourth beat of bar two should be lowered behind the heel of the left foot in the fifth position left. The dancers will then make a half-turn, bending both knees, so as to remain still in the fifth position, but with the right foot foremost. They will then be ready to pass back into their own places with 3 more hopped singles (r.l.r.) and a half-turn as before.

The reverence: This occurs in the interlacing figure in the quadernaria measure. After the 3 doubles (passing round the lady), the dancer touches or takes her right hand. On the first beat of the bar he advances the left foot a few inches; on the second beat he draws it back behind the right, inclining the head and body. On the third beat, he bends the left knee, throwing all the weight on to the left foot. On the fourth beat, restoring the weight on to the right foot, he joins the left foot to the right, in the first position, rising on the toes, with head and body erect, and sinking the heels at the close.

The left sideways double: This double is performed by the second and third man when making way for the leader, who is about to pay homage to their own rightful partner. It occupies 1 bar, as does the forward double. On the first beat, step sideways on the flat of the left foot, and on the second beat, pass the right foot behind the left, rising on the toes. On the third beat, step once again leftwards on the flat of the left foot, and on the fourth beat, join the right foot to the left, in the first position, rising on the toes. Sink the heels at the close.

LA GELOSIA

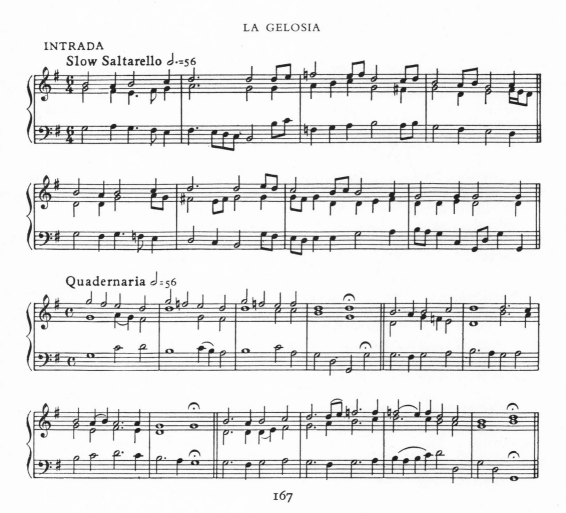

Thus, starting from the medieval treatise of Domenichino, we are able to trace the course of this grand school of dancing which, emerging from the mists of a remote past, blossomed and flourished throughout the fifteenth and sixteenth centuries in Spain and Italy. Neither does its influence appear to have declined abruptly with the dawn of the seventeenth century, at least in conservative Spain, for we find that Juan de Esquivel in his *Discursos sobre el Arte del Dançado* (Sevilla, 1642) writes as though the *Pavan, Galliard, Almain, Canaries, Torch Dance (Hachas)* and *Barriera (Torneo)* were still commonly danced in his time. The *Piva*, however, seems to have gone out of use (in connection with court dances) early in the sixteenth century, to be replaced by Galliards and Canaries. It still appears in the interesting collection of dance suites in lute tablature, published by Joan Ambrosio Dalza (Venice, 1508), which suites consist for the most part of a *Pavana, Salta-rello* and *Piva*.

The fundamental steps enumerated and explained by Domenichino, Guglielmo and Cornazano continued in use right through the fifteenth and sixteenth centuries and beyond, but with the addition of various elaborations, evolved by the later masters. Such have acquired varied and somewhat cumbrous names, differing sometimes between one master and another. To spare the student unnecessary bewilderment, I have in some cases reverted to the basic name, adding some qualifying adjective.

We are deeply indebted to the two great Italian authorities on dancing of the sixteenth century, Cesare Negri and Fabritio Caroso, for their detailed description of the dances and balletti of their own time. Both were born early in the century and both survived into the following century. Caroso was born in 1527 and Negri (supposing him to have been at least 20 when he took over the school of dancing in Milan) about 1534. Their meticulous description of the steps in use and of the airs and graces which should accompany them is also admirable.

GENTLEMAN PRACTISING CABRIOLES

Negri contributes a list of thirty-six famous dancers of his own century, with a short description of each, and of the manner in which they excelled. His longest paragraph is devoted to his own revered master, from whom he took over the Milanese school of dancing in 1554. This person, named Pompeo Diobono, journeyed in that year to France, where he became attached to the French Court. Here he was appointed by Henri II to be tutor to his second son (afterwards Charles IX). He received for this a salary of 200 francs. He was also appointed *valletto di camera*, for which he was allotted 260 francs. In addition, he received 1,000 francs for maintenance and another 160 francs for his clothes, and (over and above) was the recipient of an incalculable number of valuable presents ('ne potrei così tosto annoverar i gran presenti, che da diversi Principi furongli in poco tempo fatti').

Another Milanese dancer (Virgilio Bracesco) was the instructor of the monarch, Henri II, we are told, and also of his eldest son, the Dauphin. These curious details serve to reveal the high esteem in which the Art of Dancing was held in those picturesquely sumptuous times.

Having accorded to all these great dancers their meed of praise, Negri speaks with modesty of his own achievements, and compiles a list of the notable people before whom he has danced. From this imposing collection we may content ourselves with a few outstanding examples, namely: Queen Margherita of Spain, the Princes Ridolfo and Ernesto (sons of the Emperor Maximilian), to whom he taught *molto belle cosi* (for which service he was richly compensated), and Don Giovanni of Austria. The last-named was an enthusiastic patron of the Arts, and particularly of music and dancing. Having developed a strong affection for Negri, he used to take him with him on board ship, when he went on his expeditions against the Turkish pirates, so that he might be entertained with his dancing in between the fighting.

Caroso appears to have been a fine musician as well as a poet and dancer. It has been remarked by certain writers that, in some cases, Caroso has written his tunes in one key and the lute accompaniments in another. But this is not so. In those times, lutes of different registers were in use (treble, alto, tenor and bass), so that, although the tenor was the most favoured for solo playing, any other of these four might have been intended, of which circumstance the tablature gives no indication.

Caroso's first treatise is affectionately dedicated to 'Bianca Cappello de Medici', Grand Duchess of Tuscany, to whom he addresses four sonnets and four madrigals, and in honour of whom he presents the first two dances in the book. Many other sonnets are sprinkled through the volume, apparently all written by himself, as preludes to the individual dedications to other members of royal and noble families, both Spanish and Italian. There are also five sonnets addressed to 'the author' (written by other people).

His second treatise, *Nobilita dei Dame* (1600), is largely a revision of the first, with many helpful explanations and corrections, plus some additional complications in the matter of names of steps. This second treatise, he likens to the young bear in the fable, which, although at birth an uncouth and ugly little monster, was so tended and licked and groomed by its devoted parent that it eventually developed into a most beautiful and perfect creature.

Of all the authorities quoted in the present volume, I would say that it is the first (Domenichino) and the last-mentioned (Caroso) who are the most musical and poetic writers, on the important subject of bodily grace, consisting of a supple co-ordination of movement between the body and the feet and a sensitive emphasizing of the rhythm by some small gesture of head or hand and even, one might say, of facial expression. These 'fantasmatic shades', as Cornazano terms them, are the soul of the Dance, making of it a living thing and a true interpretation of the music of which it is the offspring.

And now I would like to reproduce for my readers a charming sonnet addressed to myself in my younger years, which gave much pleasure to Arnold Dolmetsch, through whose inspiration this work of reviving the beautiful dances of past centuries was originally undertaken.

À LA SEÑORA DE DOLMETSCH BAILANDO

Esta no es la forma de ninguna hada
Bailando bajo arboles vaporosos,
Ni ninfa que en selves lujuriantes
Juega con sus bellas trenzas de oro:—
Mas bien, es la figura
De mujer encantadora,
Llena de energía
De mística alegría
Que hace del dia un paraiso
Y de la noche un bendito sueno.

F. L. B.

Bibliography

DOMENICO DA PIACENZA. 1416. MS. *De arte Saltandi & choreas discendi.*

GUGLIELMI HEBRAEI. *c.* 1463. MS. *De pratica seu arte tripudii vulghare opusculum.* (Bibliothèque Nationale, Paris.)

   ,,   ,,   *c.* 1450–63. Five other versions of the same treatise. (In Florence, Foligno, Sienna, Modena and Paris. MSS.)

ANTONIO CORNAZANO. 1455–65. MS. *Libro dell' Arte Danzare.* (Vatican library.)

JOAN AMBROSIO DA PESARO. *c.* 1475. Manuscript copy of treatise by Guglielmi. (Bibliothèque Nationale, Paris.)

JOAN AMBROSIO DALZA. 1508. *Intabulatora di Lauto.*

FABRITIO CAROSO. 1581. *Il Ballarino.*

   ,,   ,,   1600. *Nobilita dei Dame.*

Straloch Lute Book. c. 1600. Manuscript copy of same.

THOINOT ARBEAU. 1587. *Orchésographie.*

CESARE NEGRI. 1604. *Nuove Inventione di Balli.*

JUAN DE ESQUIVEL. 1647. *Discursos sobre el Arte del Danadoç.* Madrid.

F. GREGOROVIUS. 1875. *Lucretia Borgia.*

A. LUZZIO. 1887. *I Precettori de Isabella d'Este.*

LAURE FONTA. 1888. Preface to reprint of *Orchésographie* (Arbeau).

JULIA CARTWRIGHT. 1903. *Isabella d'Este.*

Index